GREEK AND ROMAN COINS
and the Study of History

GREEK AND ROMAN COINS
and the Study of History

by
J. G. MILNE, M.A., D.Litt.

*Late Reader in Numismatics in the
University of Oxford*

GREENWOOD PRESS, PUBLISHERS
WESTPORT, CONNECTICUT

124337

Originally published in 1939
by Methuen & Company, Ltd., London

First Greenwood Reprinting 1971

Library of Congress Catalogue Card Number 75-109793

SBN 8371-4283-0

Printed in the United States of America

PREFACE

The object of this book is to suggest to teachers of ancient history what kinds of information can be derived from coins for the purpose of their work: other classes of documents and objects have been utilized to this end, but coins have been, comparatively, neglected. Professor Percy Gardner indicated the main lines of approach to be followed in the introduction to his *History of Greek Coinage*; but this did not deal with Roman coins, nor with the Hellenistic period, and the important subject of hoards and their meaning was outside his plan. Sir George Hill's *Handbook of Greek and Roman Coins* is still invaluable, and if it could have been revised to include some of the more important developments of numismatic theory in the last forty years, such as Sir George Macdonald's work on coin types, the chief need of teachers would have been met; but I understand that there is no hope of this.

The suggestions made are the result of personal experience in teaching University students, and of discussions with other teachers; but in teaching what is one man's meat is another man's poison, and every teacher must choose his own line. So I have not gone into much detail, but recorded what I have found most profitable to myself and to my pupils,

PREFACE

which others may use as a starting point for developing their own schemes. As most of the interpretations mentioned here have been argued out in papers published previously, these have only been summarized and references given to them: to add all the facts on which they are based would occupy too much space, especially in the section on hoards, which contains the impressions derived from examination of many thousands of coins.

Those who have helped me, wittingly or unwittingly, are so many that I can only express my thanks to them collectively: many, I hope, will recognize their contributions. But there are two to whom I owe a special debt, which I cannot now acknowledge to them personally: Alan Blakeway, but for whose stimulating comradeship this book might never have taken shape; and Robert Beaumont, whose share is only less because our association was even more abruptly ended.

J. G. M.

CONTENTS

*The plates, together with a key, will be found at the end
of the book.*

I. INTRODUCTORY

1. A difficulty is sometimes found in the use of Greek coins for the purpose of illustrating or explaining history, which is due to changes in the function of coinage as currency since the Greeks first developed their system. In the modern world a coin is as a rule a mere token: its purchasing power depends, not on its intrinsic value as metal, but on the denomination attached to it by the authority which issued it: this denomination is of course legally valid only in the district controlled by that authority, but may be recognized elsewhere, subject to such modifications as are imposed to meet the costs of exchange. Since comparatively little settlement of extra-territorial debts is effected by the transfer of coined money, the metal contents of a coin have no more importance for foreign business than for the home market, and it is rare to find a modern coin which would be valued as metal at anything like the figure given to it as its denomination. Even the gold coinage which was the basis of exchange in this country till recently, and which was supposed to contain its nominal value in metal, only performed this function in virtue of the price of the metal being artificially fixed, at a level above that which would be naturally determined by the costs of production and marketing:

arrangements were made for buying any gold that was offered at this artificial price, and thus what was practically a world-price for gold was maintained, until the time came when customers were found who were ready to pay a still higher price: then the so-called British gold standard broke down.

2. In Greece, on the other hand, coinage began as a convenient form of handling certain commodities for purposes of barter, and in interstate trade at any rate it never lost this character. The earliest coins were nothing more than ingots of 'pale gold' or of silver, which bore the stamp of the maker as a guarantee of quality: the irregularity of their weights shows clearly that their exact contents were not the primary consideration: the merchant made up his metal in a handy lump and exchanged it at the best price he could get. At a later stage definite values were attached to the coins, and stamps were added to show these values—the stamp of the authority which issued the coin and dictated its denomination, and in some cases secondary stamps indicating what that denomination was fòr a particular coin. This of course tended to bring the coins into the category of tokens, in their home states: if a piece of metal received the stamp which indicated that it was issued as a drachma by the governing body of a city, it was immaterial, for the purposes of trade in that city, what its metal value was; and in some places plated coins were officially struck simultaneously with those

of good metal, while in many there is evidence to be found in the coins themselves that the mint-masters paid little regard to the weight of the coins they issued. But for purposes of foreign trade the maintenance of the standard of the coinage was still a matter of importance: payments might have to be made for the settlement of debts abroad in actual cash, which would be taken at its bullion value, not at its local face value, for which purpose the purity of the coinage had to be kept up; and in the leading silver-marketing cities, notably Athens, whose silver was one of its chief articles of export, exactitude in the weight of the silver stater, which was virtually an ingot for this service, would naturally tend to increase its popularity in foreign markets. Hence in the coinages of the commercial cities the stater never became a token, so long as they preserved their autonomy; and this reacted on other cities, and helped to maintain the intrinsic value of the silver currency.

3. It is probable that the first coins to which a denomination was attached were those of the Mermnad kings of Lydia, from whose territory the alloy of gold and silver now called electrum was derived. This had been the material of numerous ingots produced by the merchants of the Greek cities of Western Asia Minor; but it is impossible to group these into any series of such homogeneity of weight as to suggest that they were intended to conform to a common standard, and the stamps on them appear to be simply

the signets of the makers, who obviously would not be in a position to enforce the acceptance of their coins at a fixed rate. The kings of Lydia, on the other hand, would be in such a position, not only in virtue of their sovereign powers in their own realms, but because the metal came from their country and would doubtless be a royal monopoly, as precious metals have been in nearly all monarchical countries throughout history; so that they could fix the selling price at the source. In view of this, it is not surprising that the first instance of what can be described as a series of electrum coins, in which considerable numbers of coins are known bearing the same badge, and falling into weight-groups which evidently represent successive fractions of the same unit, is one which, by the occurrence on some of the coins of a legend in Lydian characters, is shown to be Lydian, and which has as its type a lion's head, a badge traditionally associated with the Mermnad dynasty.

4. The idea of attaching a denomination to a coin would not make much practical appeal to the Ionian merchants, who could not control the price of their raw metal: but it was adopted on the west of the Aegaean by a ruler who was in a position to dictate the value of his money amongst a considerable clientage, and also to complete arrangements for securing a supply of metal at monopoly rates. The Aeginetan merchants had followed the example of

4

the Ionians by making up metal—silver in this case, in place of electrum—into handy ingots, and stamping these with their badge; but there is no evidence that these were, in the first instance, related to the system of currency which was generally used in Greece, a token currency represented by small iron rods. Pheidon tyrant of Argos, according to a tradition which seems to be well-founded, ordered that the Aeginetan ingot should be accepted as the equivalent of two handfuls of iron rods, and so demonetized the rods in the greater part of the Peloponnesus, which was economically dependent on Argos. The profits which would naturally accrue from this measure led to its being copied by other Greek states, each of which adjusted its coinage-unit to suit the local value of silver; and about half a century after the reform of Pheidon a further step was taken by Solon at Athens in the institution of a special system of weights for coinage, related to the old commercial weights in a manner similar to the relation of English Troy weights to avoirdupois, except that at Athens the common starting-point was at the top of the scale, in the talent; in the English it is at the bottom, in the grain.

5. The various Greek weight-standards will be discussed in detail later; but it may be noted here that the differences in standard probably arose from the circumstances of the cities concerned at the time of the institution of the coinage, especially the degree

to which they could control the price of silver: for
instance, Athens had silver-mines in its own territory,
and soon after the first issue of its coins worked them
as state property, so naturally desired to sell its silver
at the best price obtainable: Aegina depended on
silver from outside sources, mainly from Siphnos,
and wanted to get it cheap: this may be the reason
why the drachma, as a coin-weight, was fifty per cent
heavier at Aegina than at Athens. Corinth, again,
got its silver from outside, but from 'barbarian'
tribes, amongst whom the drachma would have no
meaning, as it had at Siphnos: so, when determining
their standard, the Corinthians did not need to consider the implications it might have in the minds of
the miners of the silver, and settled their price to
Greek markets as vendors. There were doubtless
other factors affecting the standards adopted at
different cities: this is cited as an example of the
problems that have to be faced in the investigation
of the origin of Greek coin-weights.

6. There is not the same difficulty in determining
the meaning of the Roman standards: at Rome the
idea of coinage was adopted from neighbouring
Italian states, which had reached a fairly advanced
stage in the development of currency. There is
hardly a trace of the use at Rome of the bronze ingots
or bars which occur freely in Etruria and Aemilia,
and the first Roman coins belong definitely to the
class which passed at face-value, each coin having its

denomination marked upon it. These were all of bronze, the normal basis of exchange in Central Italy: shortly afterwards silver coins were struck, for purposes of trade with Greek states which were accustomed to a silver standard; but these were given no official denomination, and were rated at their metal value in comparison with the bronze. They never became units of currency at Rome itself, and after fifty years were superseded when the Romans commenced to base their currency on silver, striking silver coins with a face value stated upon them as multiples of the old bronze unit: thereupon the Roman system of coinage became what it remained till the end of the Western Empire, a token coinage which expressed values derived from a bronze standard in silver, very much in the same way as the English coinage of the nineteenth century expressed in gold values derived from sterling, a standard originally silver.

II. MATERIALS

1. The materials used for purposes of currency in trade at any given place and time are important in connexion with the teaching of history, both as evidence of the economic conditions which existed, and because of the influence which they often exerted on state policy. To some extent the choice of materials for the coinage of a state was affected, in the period before the rise of great empires, by the character and direction of its foreign trade: the problem of supplies of metal was, in Greece itself, a still more serious factor in determining the relations of a city-state with its neighbours. Athens was the one city-state which had mines of a precious metal within its borders, sufficiently productive to control the market: other cities had to depend on supplies from outside their territory; and this involved, in addition to questions of competition between purchasers in the mining districts, the necessity of securing a safe transit from mine to mint. The vital importance to Athens of ensuring the arrival of supplies of corn is familiar; but it is not usually realized that Corinth was as vitally concerned in ensuring supplies of silver as well as of corn. The policy of Athens in the middle of the fifth century B.C., and the strategy of the early years of the Peloponnesian war, can best be explained

as based on the design of cutting off the supplies to Corinth of corn from the west and of silver from the north. In the world empire of Rome these political considerations did not operate to any serious extent.

GOLD

2. The use of pure gold for the purposes of currency did not become common in the Greek world until the fourth century B.C.: the metal seems to have been little used in any form on the west of the Aegaean before the middle of the sixth century, and only came gradually into favour for articles of luxury. This is in noticeable contrast to the extent to which it had been employed by the Mycenaeans, who inherited in this respect Minoan traditions: the reason for the change may have been in part the comparative poverty of the Greek communities after the Dorian invasion and the absence of any important courts or ruling houses, but a contributing cause was probably that there was no supply of gold readily available. The Mycenaeans may have got their gold from Thasos, which is reported to have had mines in early times: these were said to have been exploited by the Phoenicians, and the mention of Phoenicians in Greek legends of prehistoric times often indicates the Minoans of Crete: but the Thasian mines had probably been worked out before the main development of Greek commerce with the north of the Aegaean, and no other mines are known to have existed in or near the

9

peninsula. It is certain that when the system of coinage was adopted in Greece, none of the leading commercial cities controlled a supply of gold; consequently, there was no inducement to any to use it in the form of coin: gold imported from abroad to Athens or any other city would not appreciate in value by being stamped with the badge of the city, and it would be marketed as bullion, since the general level of prices in Greece would not require currency of high denominations for internal trade.

3. The first pure gold coinage known to the Greeks was that of Croesus, who substituted a bimetallic currency of gold and silver for the electrum of his predecessors: his gold staters were the models for the darics of the Persian kings, which dominated the Greek market for nearly two centuries. The Persian 'archers' were familiar objects in Greece in the fifth century, and they are found as far west as Sicily: in the east a hoard of darics has been found in India, though, as they were melted down, the date of the hoard cannot be determined. The introduction of gold to Greek trade from Asia probably led to the development of competing mines at points nearer the markets, of which the most important was probably Mount Pangaeus in Thrace. The gold from this field does not seem to have been exploited in the sixth century, as only silver mines are mentioned amongst the resources of Myrcinus, the nearest depot, in the time of Darius; but towards the end of the

fifth century gold coins were struck at Thasos, doubtless of metal obtained from the Pangaean mines. It
is not improbable that the opening up of these mines
was somewhat earlier, during the Athenian occupation
of the Strymon valley: in this case the gold would
have been marketed in bars or ingots, as gold formed
no part of the Athenian system of currency before the
Peloponnesian war, and the Athenians would not
want to start a gold coinage of their own, which
might have led to the depreciation of their silver in
foreign markets. When, however, the Athenian
control of the Thraceward parts was relaxed after
the loss of Amphipolis, it would be to the advantage
of the Thasians, to whom the shipping of the produce
of the mines would naturally pass, to turn the gold
into coin and sell it at the best rate they could, regardless of Athenian regulations.

4. About the same time as that at which the
Thasian gold coinage commenced, the exigencies of
war led to the issue of small gold pieces in several
cities: at Camarina, Gela, and Acragas such pieces are
known, which were almost certainly struck when
these cities were besieged by the Carthaginians in
the campaigns of 406 and 405, and similar pieces
from Syracuse may belong either to these years or
to the Athenian siege nine years earlier. At Athens
it is known that during the closing stage of the Peloponnesian war, in 407, gold objects were melted down
to be turned into coin, and the coins struck then have

been identified. But these temporary expedients would hardly lead to the more general use of gold as currency in Greece: and the fact that in the first quarter of the fourth century a number of issues of gold appeared in various parts of Greece is rather to be ascribed to the growing employment of mercenary troops by the states. Many of the mercenaries might have seen service in Asia and have become accustomed there to be paid in gold: the most extensive of these issues, with one exception, was at Syracuse, where the mercenary soldier was a familiar figure during the reign of Dionysius.

5. The exceptional issue of gold was that of the city of Lampsacus, which seems to have been a definitely commercial venture; the choice of types and the general style of the coins suggest that they were intended to compete with the electrum staters struck at the neighbouring mint of Cyzicus. For over a century the Cyzicene staters had played a very important part in Greek inter-state trade, serving as a medium of exchange for high values between the Asiatic cities, whose currency was ultimately based on the Persian gold standard, and the European, whose standards were all silver: it would seem that the authorities at Lampsacus had realized that gold was coming into more common use as a factor in international business, and so tried to supplant the Cyzicenes with a more up-to-date set of coins. They certainly succeeded in getting a wide circulation

for their gold, which is found all over the Greek world, though it did not drive the Cyzicenes off the field: Cyzicenes and Lampsacenes are found associated together in fourth century hoards. It is not probable that either set of staters was given a definite denomination at its city of origin: the coins were intended for external use, and would be valued in terms of silver drachmas according to the relative values of the metals at whatever city they happened to be marketed, and these varied considerably: for instance, a Cyzicene stater was worth 28 drachmas at Athens, but only $21\frac{2}{3}$ at Panticapaeum in the Crimea, in the middle of the fourth century.

6. The gold for the Lampsacene issues was probably obtained from South Russia, where the Greek settlers at Panticapaeum began to coin gold staters about the same time as the city of Lampsacus. Considerable numbers of these staters have been found in the Black Sea area, but they do not appear to have reached Greece, and it may be surmised that they were recoined at Lampsacus: the only specimen recorded as found outside the Hellespont is one in a hoard of some thousands of gold coins from Sidon. The Panticapaean stater weighed 140 grains, and the Lampsacene 130, so the weights are consistent with the theory of recoinage.

7. The position of gold in the Greek monetary system was entirely altered when Philip II of Macedon issued an extensive series of gold coins with a fixed

relation of value to his silver coinage: he controlled supplies of both metals from his mines in Mount Pangaeus, and so was able to adjust his prices to those of the leading Greek markets: he adopted the Athenian ratio of 10:1, and thus undersold the Persian daric and captured the gold trade of European Greece. His dual coinage of gold and silver was developed and extended by Alexander III, and their issues dominated the gold circulation of the Greek world till the establishment of the Roman Empire. The earlier Hellenistic kings struck some quantity of gold, and a few of the city states added to the supply: but the main stock of gold coin in Greece must have been the staters of Alexander, at any rate down to the middle of the second century, after which there is comparatively little evidence of the use of gold in Greece: the Roman conquests of the first half of that century had drained a large quantity of the metal to Italy, and there was no ruler or city of the Greek world who was in a position to replenish the stock.

8. The Romans did not use the gold that they exacted from the Greeks for coinage: the mint of Rome produced no gold coins under the Republic, except for some small emergency issues in times of war, and the few gold pieces that are regarded as belonging to the Roman series were issued elsewhere by Roman commanders for military occasions. During the Civil Wars the coinage of denarii aurei became more frequent, but most of these were struck

in the East: it was left for Augustus to systematize the currency and to adopt gold as an integral part of the Roman circulation. Even then the Imperial mint for gold was not at Rome, but at Lugdunum, and it was only in the course of the first century A.D. that the issue was concentrated at Rome. But the Romans never based their currency on gold: the 'denarius aureus' was only a multiple of the silver denarius, and as this was in its turn an expression in silver of a multiple of the bronze as, the values were unstable: it was not till the reign of Anastasius that the first real gold standard was introduced.

ELECTRUM

9. The natural alloy of gold and silver known amongst the Greeks officially as pale gold, and later popularly called electrum, which was found in Lydia, was, as has been mentioned already, the first material used by the Greeks for coinage, in the sense that lumps of metal were made up in a size convenient for trade and stamped with a badge or trade-mark as a guarantee of quality. This practice was begun by the Greek merchants of western Asia Minor, who may have inherited the idea from their Mycenaean ancestors, and borrowed from them by the kings of Lydia, to whom the invention of coinage was ascribed in later times, probably because they were the first to fix currency values for their coins. The Lydian coinage vanished with the fall of the kingdom: but

the Greek cities of the Asiatic coast continued to strike electrum for foreign trade, and after the sixth century the issue of coins in this metal was almost entirely concentrated at the three cities of Cyzicus, Phocaea, and Mytilene. These coins were apparently issued under some common understanding between the cities: an agreement governing the striking of coins by Phocaea and Mytilene in alternate years is preserved in an inscription; and, as the whole of the electrum coinage of those two cities consists of sixths, while Cyzicus produced mainly staters, it is probable that there was a division of functions made by joint consent: the staters appear to have been known in popular usage as Cyzicenes, the sixths as Phocaides, regardless of where they were struck. There is no evidence that any of these coins was given a denomination in ordinary terms of Greek currency by its issuers: they were always staters or fractions of staters, not drachmas or multiples of drachmas. The metal seems to have been struck as it came to the market, without regard to the proportionate content of gold and silver, which varied considerably, so far as can be tested by the specific gravity of the coins: probably it was accepted as a distinct metal, not as a mixture of gold and silver, and the values of its component parts did not enter into account.

10. For the greater part of the Greek world the utility of the electrum coinage ceased with the establishment of the Empire of Alexander, and the

MATERIALS

Asiatic mints closed: but in the West, outside the
Empire, a good deal of electrum was struck. This
was probably an artificial alloy, and should be regarded
rather as a debased gold coinage than as an independent one: the earliest examples are from Syracuse,
issued in the middle of the fourth century under Dion,
whose circumstances might well lead to a debasement
of the currency. The plentiful electrum coinage of
Carthage, which began not long afterwards, may be
ascribed to the same causes: and here a depreciation
in the silver as well as in the gold can be traced. A
similar history of degradation occurs in the coinage
of the client kings of Bosporus under the Roman
Empire, which began with gold staters, rapidly depreciating to electrum: in the third century they were
merely billon and ended in the middle of the fourth
as bronze. The gold coinage of the late Byzantine
Emperors followed much the same course, through
electrum to bronze.

SILVER

11. Silver was the one precious metal which
could be obtained in quantity from mines in or near
the Greek peninsula, and was the standard of all early
currencies in that region. It does not seem to have
been much used by the Mycenaeans, who may have
preferred gold for their decorative work, and had
no metal currency so far as is known. The development of the Greek silver trade may be dated to the

17

end of the eighth century, and probably resulted from the discovery that there was a steady demand for silver in Egypt: the Aeginetans, the chief maritime merchants of Greece, had begun to take a share in the Egyptian trade which had been started by the Ionians, possibly on the suggestion of Minoan and Mycenaean tradition handed down from their ancestors, and would quickly realize that Egypt would pay a much higher price for silver than any Greek state. The Aeginetans had supplies of silver close at hand, and adopted the Ionian method of marketing the metal in stamped ingots of small size for convenience of handling: so, soon after 700 B.C., the Aeginetan silver staters made their appearance, in the first instance probably valued only at metal rates as bullion for export. About 650 Pheidon of Argos took in hand the reform of the media of exchange in Greece, presumably to facilitate trade between the cities: he adopted the silver of Aegina, which, if not the only currency of the kind in Greece, was the only important one, as the basis for his reform, and followed the precedent set by the Lydian kings by giving it a fixed denomination in terms of the native Greek unit of value, the drachma. The drachma had been represented by a bundle of iron rods, from which it got its name—virtually a token currency: the Aeginetan stater could apparently be bought for two such bundles in the Argive market, since it was treated as a didrachm: and this new currency rapidly superseded

18

the old one in most of the markets of Greece. Other commercial centres, such as Corinth and Chalcis, realized the advantages of this system and started rival issues of their own, on standards suited to their local conditions, but always on a silver basis: and thereafter silver was the sole monetary medium of nearly all the states of Greece till the close of the fifth century, and always remained the standard.

12. There were numerous places in the Greek area where silver was mined, but the most important in historic times belonged to four groups. The earliest mines to be developed were those of the islands of the Aegaean, especially Siphnos, which probably reached its maximum of productivity in the seventh and sixth centuries: during this period its trade was under the control of Aegina, and the silver was probably all marketed at Aegina and sold at prices fixed by the Aeginetan ring of merchants. After the Persian wars Siphnos disappears from the scene, and it may be assumed that the mines were exhausted. The first alternative supply that was tapped by Greek traders was from Paeonia, where there were extensive mining areas in the upper valley of the Axius: these seem to have been known to Corinthian merchants in the middle of the seventh century, when the metal was brought south along the old overland route past Dodona. Before the end of the century, however, other routes were opened, one down the Axius valley to the Thermaic gulf, where Euboean and Corinthian

colonies were established to serve as depots for the shipment of the metal, the other through the hills westwards to the Adriatic, where it was handled by the Corcyraeans and Corinthians. Silver continued to be derived from this district till the Middle Ages, and the workings can still be seen. The mines at Laureium in Attica were probably not developed till the sixth century, and possibly the first systematic exploitation there was due to Pisistratus: the richest veins were reached in the early years of the fifth century. They were always under the control of Athens, and throughout the period of Athenian autonomy were one of the main sources of the wealth of the city; but there is evidence that they were becoming less productive in the first century B.C., and there is practically no trace of operations in them under the Roman Empire. The fourth group of mines may have been worked a little earlier than those of Laureium: this was in Thrace, to the east of the Strymon, on and near Mount Pangaeus: in the beginning the silver was probably won by the native tribes and marketed at Thasos, whence it was shipped to Ionia and so to Egypt: the Persian conquest of Thrace diverted the supply to the treasury of the Great King for a few years, till the retreat of the Persians from Europe gave the King of Macedonia the chance of securing the mines. The Athenians tried to get control of them, and for a brief period succeeded in establishing themsevles at Amphipolis, which was the key position of the district; but when they were expelled from Amphipolis after the victory of Brasidas, the mines reverted to the Macedonian kings, and in the middle of the fourth century were probably the most productive in the Greek world during the intensive operations of Philip II. They were still worked in the second and first centuries, but it is doubtful whether they continued under the Roman Empire: when the silver had to be sent to Rome to be coined, it would probably be cheaper for the Romans to get their supply from Spain.

13. Silver from outside the Balkan peninsula does not seem to have affected the metal market in Greece to any great extent. The Persian kings probably derived their chief supplies from further east, and, though their sigloi were current throughout Asia Minor, it was only at a few cities on the coast that they influenced the exchange rates: they did not cross the Aegaean, like the gold darics. In the far west, the silver mines of Spain had become known to the Ionians in the seventh century, and there is considerable evidence of Greek trade with Spain about 600: but after the rise of Carthage as an independent state, instead of a colony of Tyre, in the middle of the sixth century, direct communication between Greece and Spain was stopped by the joint action of the Carthaginians and the Etruscans. Thereafter Spanish silver went in the first instance to Carthage, and possibly to Etruria: it did filter into Greek lands

through border markets such as Himera and Selinus in Sicily and Cumae in Campania, and had some influence on values in their neighbourhood, but this was only of local importance: the silver coinage struck for the Carthaginian stations in Sicily was modelled on the Greek coinages which it was intended to rival, and did not affect the standard of the leading Greek issues of Sicily.

14. The Spanish silver mines became dominant in the Mediterranean world after the Romans had conquered Spain. The first Roman coins were struck for military purposes, on Greek models and probably from Greek silver: then a more extensive series was produced, which could be used for foreign exchange at bullion values, but had no fixed relation to Roman currency: finally, when the output of Spain was at their disposal, the Romans adopted silver as their medium of exchange and tried to express the denominations of their old bronze standard in that metal. Till the end of the second century A.D., if not longer, Spain seems to have been the principal Roman source of silver: the Illyrian mines were second in importance, and lesser supplies were derived from other provinces; but, as the only mint for striking silver in Europe was at Rome, from the middle of the first century A.D. to the end of the second, there would have been no advantage for purposes of coinage in going far afield in search of metal.

MATERIALS

15. Copper never took more than a subsidiary place in the currency of Greece: it was familiar enough as a metal, and bronze articles had, according to tradition, been used as one of the measures of exchange in the Heroic Age, though there is no certain evidence, except possibly in Crete, of similar use in historic times. As has been seen, the origin of coinage in Greece was probably due to the demand for silver in foreign countries, and there was no similar demand for Greek copper or bronze which would lead to the metal being made up into stamped ingots like those of silver: the local production of copper in Greece was probably not more than sufficient for local requirements. It was not till the use of coin in the ordinary business of life in the Greek cities had become familiar to the citizens, and the inconvenience of handling minute silver coins for the payment of small sums had suggested the desirability of substituting some less valuable metal for low denominations of currency, that a bronze coinage made its appearance in the Greek peninsula: this took place about 400 B.C., and probably began at Athens, but rapidly spread throughout the land.

16. Coins of bronze, had, however, been struck by some of the Greek cities of Sicily a good deal earlier than this, probably soon after 480: these were intended for use in trade with the inhabitants of the interior of the island, predominantly tribes of Italian

23

origin, who may have brought with them the Italian tradition of making copper, a metal more easily obtained than silver in Italy, their standard of exchange. The earliest of the Sicilian bronze coins were of a fabric which was not Greek in appearance, and on a system of values based on the Italian litra of twelve unciae: this was related to the Greek silver drachma at rates which varied according to the local exchanges of the cities concerned. The fabric gradually became more Greek in the course of the fifth century, but the dual system of the drachma and the litra continued till the drachma was finally ousted by the Roman denarius.

17. The only other instance of a bronze standard in the Greek world—if an exceptional set of bronze coins issued on the north of the Euxine at Olbia may be disregarded as scarcely Greek—is found in Egypt under Ptolemaic rule. Before the conquest of Egypt by Alexander the use of silver as a measure of value in business does not seem to have been known: values were stated in gold or copper, both of which were obtainable on the borders of Egypt, in Nubia and Sinai respectively; while silver had to be imported from a distance, mainly, as already mentioned, from Greece, and was consequently more costly in terms of gold or copper in Egypt than in most countries round the Mediterranean. So long as the empire of Alexander subsisted, the Egyptians had to use the same coinage as the other provinces: but, when Egypt

became a separate kingdom under Ptolemy Soter, the price of silver naturally appreciated to something like its old relation to gold; and, after some endeavours to maintain the silver drachma as a basis of currency by lowering its content, Ptolemy Philadelphus, about 270, introduced a bronze drachma, which rapidly became the regular measure of values for internal trade in Egypt. Thenceforward, till the Roman conquest of Egypt, the only silver coins struck by the Ptolemies were for their outlying possessions, Cyprus and, in the third century, Phoenicia: base silver tetradrachms were issued and used in Egypt itself, but their silver content dropped during the second century to about twenty-five per cent, and in external markets they were only taken at a quarter of their nominal value. The official ratio of the silver drachma to the bronze during this period was 480 to 1, or about four times that which prevailed elsewhere in the Mediterranean area.

18. Rome, on the other hand, began its coinage on a bronze standard, following Italian tradition: bars or ingots of bronze were the earliest form of currency known in Central Italy, and the custom of casting round coins of bronze probably began in Etruria about the end of the fifth century, and was copied in Umbria, Picenum, and Latium. So, when in 289 the Romans appointed officials to produce a coinage, they naturally adopted the same idea and based their system of values on a bronze unit, the as,

which continued to be the nominal basis until the end of the Roman coinage in the fifth century A.D. In 217 B.C. the authorities at Rome changed over from bronze to silver for the expression of their currency, and until the end of the Republic the use of bronze steadily diminished, hardly any being issued in the middle of the first century B.C.: under the Empire, however, it revived and continued as an essential part of the circulation.

OTHER METALS

19. Metals other than gold, silver, or copper were hardly ever used for coinage in either the Greek or the Roman system of currency. Iron, in the form of bars, had been the chief Greek medium of exchange before the monetary reform of Pheidon, but after they had been superseded by the new silver coinage the use of this metal ceased, except at Sparta: as there were iron mines in Laconia and the Spartan theory of state economics aimed at the minimum of dependence on imports, iron continued to be the measure of values at Sparta probably till the fifth century. It was not coined, but may have circulated in bars as of old: a few iron coins are found in Greece, some struck at Argos, but they were most probably emergency issues only. Lead was extensively employed in Egypt in the second and third centuries A.D. for small change: after 180 the Imperial mint at Alexandria issued hardly any coins except tetradrachms, and the needs of local

MATERIALS

business were met by the production of leaden coins, diobols and obols, in the chief towns of the country districts: many of these are of quite good workmanship and may be regarded as the issues of the town author- ities. Elsewhere in the Greek world the only leaden coins known are copies of silver or bronze types, and are either emergency issues or contemporary forgeries. The references in ancient authors to tin coinages point to the same kind of fraud, so far as Greece and Italy are concerned: the only tin coinage which can be regarded as a real circulating medium is that found in Gaul and Britain, which seems to date from the first century B.C.

III. DEBASEMENT

1. The early Greek coinages of silver and gold were struck in metal of a high grade of fineness, any impurities present being probably due rather to imperfect methods of refining than to any intention of debasement. Since in the first instance coins were made up as a convenient method of marketing a commodity, and stamped with badges as a guarantee of purity, a merchant who deliberately put out coins of a low standard of fineness would have been acting against his business interests: and when rulers and cities had given denominations to their coins, these were only valid in their own domains, outside which the coins were still taken at their bullion values. The early electrum coinage was certainly not designed as a base gold coinage, but as one in a distinct metal: the only instance of a coinage in base silver of early date is that of Lesbos, which in the fifth century struck an extensive series of billon: for this no satisfactory explanation has yet been suggested.

2. There was however an appreciable quantity of plated coinage issued in the sixth and fifth centuries, which seems to have come from official mints, since in some cases the plated coins are struck from the same dies as the good ones. The earliest reference to such a practice is in the story of Polycrates of Samos, whose

28

so-called plated gold was doubtless electrum: several examples of plated electrum sixths of fifth century date, of the Lesbian and Phocaean series, exist; and the provision in the agreement for a joint currency made by Mytilene and Phocaea, which prescribed penalties for the issue of coins below standard, was presumably aimed against such plated pieces. The coins struck by Themistocles at Magnesia, after the revenues of that city were given to him by the King of Persia, provide an example of an issue which was partly pure and partly plated; and at the end of the fifth century the cities of Phoenicia produced a good deal of plated silver. In Greece itself the Athenian coinage was of unexceptionable quality: the only plated Athenian coins in existence are the emergency issues of the siege-years at the end of the Peloponnesian War, which were redeemed as soon as possible. But in the series of Aegina and Corinth several examples of plated coins are known, which are quite as likely to have been the products of the official mints as the work of private forgers. The extent to which the practice of plating prevailed, even as early as the sixth century, may be deduced from the state of coins found in hoards of that date in Egypt: in nearly every case the coins have been chopped through, to make sure that they are not plated.

3. Official debasement became more common in Hellenistic times: not only in Egypt, where local metal prices led to the production of base silver coins, but

elsewhere in the East there is a marked deterioration of the quality of the silver. This followed naturally on the increase in the proportion of the currency which consisted of silver circulating at forced values in specie: the majority of the Hellenistic coinages are token coinages, like nearly all modern ones, and did not depend for their valuation on their metal content. In the West, especially in Italy, plating was more usual than debasement: the proportion of plated coins struck from official dies in several of the cities of Magna Graecia is considerable. The Romans learnt the practice presumably from this source, and by the end of the second century B.C. plated denarii formed a regular part of the currency of Rome. It has been suggested, and the suggestion is attractive, that sound money became a party question at Rome; the equites, since their foreign business connexions required coins whose intrinsic value bore a fair relation to their face value, endeavoured to maintain the purity of the metal, while the Senatorial leaders were content with anything that would pass at Rome so long as it furnished an immediate profit to the state.

4. There are no certain instances of plated gold coins from official dies before the time of the Roman Empire: some plated gold staters of the types of Alexander have been found in Palestine, but these are probably private forgeries. The issues of alloyed gold at Syracuse and Carthage have already been mentioned: these can be taken as examples of a deliberate

debasement by the state authorities, which were not struck from the same dies as the pure gold coins, but were intended to supersede them.

5. If the plated issues are disregarded, it may be said that the silver content of the Roman denarius was well maintained till the reign of Nero, when there was a recoinage on a lower standard: after that there was little further change till the beginning of the third century. With the introduction of the Antoninianus by Caracalla a course of depreciation began: before the middle of the century the silver denarius had ceased to be issued, and the silver in the Antoninianus became more and more exiguous, till it was the merest wash on a bronze core; this quickly wore off with handling, so that nearly all the coins of Gallienus and later Emperors appear to be bronze. The nominally silver issues of the eastern provinces lost quality in sympathy; the tetradrachms of Antioch, which were of fairly good silver at the end of the second century, had degraded to very poor billon when they ceased to be struck just after 250; and the series which continued longest, that of Alexandria, contained only traces of silver in the last thirty years before its coinage ended in 296. Plated gold coins of the Imperial types are not infrequently found, which may be official products: it is also possible that the cast denarii of base silver or tin which occur in some provinces were issues, with some sort of official sanction, made by the local authorities to meet the needs of their districts. The

transmission of supplies of cash for the payment of the troops must have been one of the principal means of putting the products of the Roman mint into circulation: if these supplies were cut off, the civilian population would soon find itself short of currency, and the local authorities would have to come to the rescue with the best substitutes they could provide. The base coinages found in the provinces may therefore be treated as emergency issues rather than as forgeries.

IV. FABRIC

1. The stamped lumps of electrum, generally regarded as the most primitive form of coinage used in Greek lands, are technically only a short step in advance of the lumps of metal found on Minoan and Mycenaean sites, which are made up to definite standards of weight, though without any stamp or mark on them. The merchants of Western Asia Minor realized the business advantage of placing the maker's mark on the metal, as a guarantee of quality, and impressed their devices on the backs of dumps of metal which had been melted and then dropped on some flat surface to cool: it would obviously be easier to handle gold in this form than as dust. Then, presumably, it was observed that the lower face of the dump took the impression of any lines that happened to be on the surface upon which it was dropped, and the idea occurred of putting the maker's mark on the dump by engraving it on that surface, so creating a kind of die: this offered a larger field for the artist, and led to more elaboration of devices. The little nail-headed punches which had been used in the first instance for impressing the marks on the back were gradually increased in size, to make the more sure of driving the metal down into all parts of the die: in these also, as the size grew, there was more opportunity

33

for engraving designs on the punches, and finally they became second dies. The lower die—the old flat surface—is usually called the anvil die, the upper the punch die.

2. An exceptional fabric is found in a group of coins struck by the Thracian tribes of the Strymon valley in the sixth century B.C.: here the flans are spread, and there is a marked difference in the relief of the designs on the two faces, that on the side from the anvil die being fairly high, while on the other side there is often a mere shadow of a design. It would seem probable that here the anvil die was of the usual type, but instead of a punch die for driving the metal home, a flat squeezer with some device sketched on it was employed: this would exert less pressure on the metal, comparatively, than a punch of a smaller area, and the result is that these coins have a surface more like that of cast than of struck pieces. A similar appearance is presented by early coins of Etruria, and the same explanation may apply there.

3. A more remarkable technical development is shown in certain coinages struck in South Italy in the sixth century, which were produced by a pair of dies with the same design on both, incuse on the anvil die and in relief on the punch die; so that, when the coin was struck, it had the type in relief on the obverse and incuse on the reverse, producing the effect of a metal plate with the design repoussé, or beaten up from the back, as in principle it was. This scheme

34

was probably adopted for artistic reasons: the designs were treated with more elaboration than on any contemporary Greek coinages, and the correspondence of the face of the punch die with that of the anvil die would secure that the type would be more thoroughly struck up in all details than could be done with the kind of punch die in general use at the period. The design was also as a rule surrounded by an intricate border, and the fitting of the two dies into one another at this border may have been intended to serve as a sort of collar to control the spread of the metal. This technique, however, was not followed outside the district in which it was invented, and died out there about the end of the sixth century: the artistic results were good, but probably it did not pay from a commercial standpoint.

4. Other mints about the same time, such as those of Corinth and some of the Sicilian cities, tried to secure the even striking of the design by broadening the face of the punch die so as to cover the whole field to which the metal would spread under pressure: this was effective with a design in shallow relief, but probably shortened the life of the dies; and, like the South Italian technique, it did not last after the sixth century. The great majority of sixth and fifth century Greek coins were struck with punch dies whose faces were smaller than the flans of the coins, so that on the reverses there is a central incuse, with the metal rising in a rim all round it.

5. In the fifth century and later it is probable that the flans of coins of the larger modules were cast before striking: this would be specially important in commercial coinages, where exactitude of weight was desirable: it would also be easier to strike large coins if the flans were already shaped, and Greek dies seem to have been rather weak. In the Ptolemaic bronze series the cast flans seem also to have been turned to a regular size before they were struck. For small silver it was apparently the practice of some mints in the Hellenistic period to use blanks stamped out of a strip of rolled metal.

6. Many of the coins produced at cities which did not control supplies of raw metal must, however, have been struck on old coins used as blanks: there is no evidence to show that silver was traded in the form of bars or similar ingots in Greece, and it seems clear that the coins must have served as ingots. If a shipment of silver had to be made from a Greek city, it would probably be composed of coins: the hoards of Greek silver found in the Levantine area, which certainly represent exports of bullion, only occasionally contain a small quantity of scrap metal with the coins; and, as these hoards were simply destined for the melting-pot, there would have been no reason for sending coins in preference to bars, if bars had existed. In these circumstances, if a city wished to have an issue of coins of its own types, it would often be the simplest plan to obtain a stock of blanks either by importing

a lot of coins from one of the great silver markets, or by collecting any coins that happened to be in circulation in the city: these coins could then be restruck after the original types had been defaced by hammering or melting. The clearest proof that this practice was followed is furnished by examples of restruck coins from various parts of the Greek world, notably South Italy, Lycia, and Crete, on which the previous types can still be traced, owing to the defacement having been imperfectly performed. Occasionally there are traces of two restrikings; and microscopical examination has shown that the crystalline structure of some Greek coins, which bore no evidence on their faces of having been subjected to such re-use, was suggestive of their having been so treated. Valuable evidence about the lines of Greek trade can be derived from these restruck coins, even when the original types cannot be identified: if such coins were collected from those in circulation in the local markets, they would be mainly what had drifted there in course of trade, and would represent the standard which was used at the headquarters of the trade. In the study of this evidence, it must be remembered that the weight would tend to have been reduced by the wear of the coins as they passed from hand to hand: thus, for instance, the average weight of the coins struck in the South Italian cities, the trade of which was dominated by Corinth, in the sixth century shows a steady drop in the stater, as the distance from Corinth increases, beginning at Tarentum and going round to Poseidonia.

7. Restriking would also be a convenient way of dealing with demonetized coins, which must have been plentiful in Greece at certain periods: so long as a city maintained its independence, its coins might be negotiated at something near their specie value among the money-changers of foreign cities: but if it lost the degree of sovereign power implicit in the issue of coins, the guarantee for the specie value vanished, and the coins would only be rated as bullion. Such coins might receive a new value in specie by being restruck with a new stamp of guarantee: that this was done is suggested, for instance, by the increase in the number of coins of weights on the Persian standard which is found in the cities of Western Asia Minor in the third century B.C., when there would be large quantities of demonetized Persian sigloi in the market; and again by the extensive issues of tetradrachms in the same district in the next century, which are mainly on blanks that are obviously hammered out of earlier coins, some certainly and others probably tetradrachms of Alexander III: their guarantee might have held good under his Successors in the third century B.C., but faded after the battle of Magnesia.

8. There is less evidence of the restriking of bronze coins than of silver in Greek lands, partly because the question of revaluation did not arise, since bronze was almost everywhere nothing but a token currency,

partly because bronze coins seldom travelled far in course of trade from their place of origin. But cities did occasionally restrike their own bronze—there is an example of this on an extensive scale at Smyrna in the first century B.C.—and that coins of different cities could be gathered for this purpose is shown by the composition of a hoard of somewhat earlier date found in the vicinity of Smyrna.

9. At Rome there is no evidence of the restriking of coins after the third century B.C., when the standard had been changed from bronze to silver. Several instances are known of Ptolemaic bronze coins being used as blanks for Roman coins, and a certain amount of bronze seems to have been restruck in various cities of South Italy during the war with Hannibal. But when silver was adopted for the expression of the currency in 217, there was no need for restriking: the central mint must always have controlled plentiful supplies of silver from the Spanish mines, which seems, unlike the Greek silver, to have been traded in bars, and no question of demonetization would trouble the authorities. Even in the last years of the Republic, rival parties seem to have accepted one another's issues without discrimination; and the coins of the seceding allies in the Social War are found in hoards mixed with Roman denarii. In the Greek provinces there was some re-using of coins in the first century of the Empire, notably in the silver cistophori of Asia Minor: these were of a standard which did not

fit conveniently into the Roman series, and seem to
have served for the purpose of propaganda, perhaps
almost as medals, rather than for purely commercial
objects: so that it would be convenient, if a fresh set
was needed, to re-use some old ones instead of prepar-
ing fresh blanks. In the third century restriking became
more common, especially in the outlying parts of
the Empire: if a provincial commander was
proclaimed Emperor, he would have any current
coins that were at hand restamped with his own
effigy and titles: occasionally the same was done for
an emperor who was fully recognized; for instance,
in the fourth century the first issues for Jovian at
Antioch included a number of coins restruck on coins
of Constantius. Then, as the hold of Rome on the
provinces weakened, and the supply of coins from the
central mints decreased, it would frequently be necessary for the local authorities, if they wanted a supply of
coins that had some recognizable guarantee, to collect
old defaced pieces and restrike them: so that the semi-
barbarous issues which appeared in several parts of
what had been Roman territory are commonly overstruck on what had once been Roman coins.

10. Greek and Roman coins are normally round
in shape: the earliest pieces had naturally taken this
form, since they were struck on lumps of metal dropped on to a flat surface, and this probably fixed the
tradition in popular use. A number of bean-shaped
coins occur, but these are rather accidental, due to the

employment of a double punch which squeezed the metal out sideways. Square coins are only found in the series issued in the far eastern provinces after the break-up of the Empire of Alexander, and are certainly due to the influence of Indian ideas: the rectangular bronze bricks of the Central Italian area can hardly be classed as coins, any more than the cast bars which preceded them as currency. In one or two outlying regions the inception of bronze coinage saw various abnormal forms, such as the fish-shaped pieces of the Euxine and the Agrigentine series of multiples of the uncia, but these had no long life. It seems to have been accepted in the Greek world that a coin ought to be round: so when in the fifth and fourth centuries the mint of Cyzicus issued electrum staters of irregular shape alongside of silver coins that were neatly rounded, an impression is produced that this was done deliberately to emphasize the fact that the staters were not coins with a denomination in specie, but bullion made up in a standard form for convenience of handling—in short, just lumps of metal.

V. DIES

1. The development of dies for use in coinage seems to have proceeded by a gradual evolution from the anvil surface and punch of the primitive electrum pieces. The designs engraved on the anvil dies were at first little more than hollows scooped in the faces, which were arranged in geometric forms that became more elaborate, and then introduced representations of some natural object: even when this stage was reached, the object was usually of the simplest character, such as the Aeginetan turtle or the Phocaean seal, which could be depicted by the employment of a single tool. When the punch was turned into a second die, the same course of development was repeated; and it was probably over a century after the appearance of engraved designs on the anvil dies that they first came into vogue on the punch dies.

2. No examples of Greek dies of the archaic period are known: the earliest that have been found are of the fifth century. As will be shown later, the dies were normally used till they broke up: if a die became obsolete while it was still in good condition, as for instance on a change in the official responsible for the coinage, whose badge or name was engraved on the die, it would sometimes be adapted for continued service by cutting a new badge or name over the old

42

one. In any case, it would have been unlikely that the authorities would allow useable dies to pass out of their keeping. It may be assumed that in the archaic period the punch and anvil dies were not mechanically connected or adjusted to one another in any way; they could be employed independently, and one punch might strike coins on several different anvils, or several punches be used on the same anvil. Also there is no evidence to show that regularly organized mints existed in Greece in the seventh century: it is possible that the striking of the coins was done by travelling silversmiths, who took their tools with them and operated at any place where they got an order, as was the practice in certain parts of India in the last century. This would explain the occurrence of coins struck with the obverse types of different cities, but with the same reverse punch. On the other hand, such combinations might result if a mint was established in a city and then struck coins for other cities, as has frequently occurred; and this seems the more probable, in view of what has been said above as to the Greek habit of trading silver in the form of coin.

3. In any case, that the dies were not adjusted is clear from the fact that specimens struck from the same pair of dies are found with the designs on the two faces of the coins in different axial relations to one another. The study of die-positions—that is, the relation of the axis of one die to that of the other on any given coin— becomes important in the fifth century, because the

practice of Greek mints at and after that time shows variations which were to some extent localized. In descriptions of coins the die-position is shown by a pair of arrows indicating the axes of the two dies, or more summarily by a single arrow for the reverse die, the obverse die being assumed to be vertical: for instance, ↑ or ↓ would mean that the two axes were in the same plane, so that if the coin was held with the obverse design vertically upright and then rotated, the reverse design would also be vertical:—→ or ←— would mean that the reverse design would be horizontal. The evidence which has been collected in this way during years shows that in the Asiatic cities and the Near East the two axes were normally in the same plane, and it would appear that some system of coupling the dies must have been devised. This scheme was most fully developed at Alexandria under the Ptolemies, and continued there after the Roman conquest: except in a period of some three years in the reign of Severus Alexander, when a foreign element was introduced, the Alexandrian mint during three centuries issued no coins that had not the two types with their axes in the same plane, and the operatives did their work so exactly that series of a dozen or more coins from the same pair of dies do not show any measurable difference in the die-positions; so that it is practically certain that at Alexandria the dies were hinged to one another. The Greek cities of Europe, on the other hand, kept to the use of free dies for a much longer time: in some cases, as at Athens, the die-positions are virtually of four varieties, $\uparrow$, $\leftarrow$, $\downarrow$, and $\rightarrow$: this is explained by the fact that the extant specimen of an Athenian die is square in section: if a square die were to be placed so that its edges were aligned to those of its mate, without regard to the position of the type engraved on the die, it is clear that the result might be any one of the four relations of the designs shown above. The same phenomenon is found in certain mediæval coinages, which are known to have been struck with square dies. Other cities, especially in the Western parts of the Greek world, did not make even this attempt at adjustment of their dies, and the designs appear at all angles to one another.

4. These differences are of importance, not only for determining the region in which a coin was struck—for instance, the coins of Alexander III were produced at mints in all parts of his empire with the same types, only differentiated by symbols in the field, the attribution of which to their mints is often not obvious, and the classification of the issues under provinces depends largely on die-positions—but also in connexion with the arrangement of the coins in chronological order, by the sequence of the dies used. A Greek die, as noted already, was normally used till it was worn out: the mint-workmen were seemingly often reluctant to throw out a die even when it had been cracked or broken: numerous cases can be

found which show a flaw in a die becoming more and more serious, until a part of the face is lost. The life of the obverse dies was as a rule much longer than that of the reverse dies: this is easily understandable, since the reverse die would be battered with blows from a hammer, while the obverse was set in an anvil or some similar support: the life of an obverse die has been calculated to have been on the average from six to seven times that of a reverse in the mint of Alexandria. In the Eastern cities, where the dies were fixed, an obverse die would be used with a succession of reverses, until it broke up: then a new obverse would be placed in the anvil, the reverse die which was the upper member of the old pair remaining. The result is that coins from a particular obverse die may be found associated with several reverses; but only about one reverse die in six will be found associated with two obverses, presumably a reverse which happened to be in use when the old obverse die broke. In such series, if a fair number of examples can be compared, it is possible to arrange the dies in chronological order by the linkings thus shown, and so to get a sequence of issues. But in the mints of Central and Western Greece, where the dies were loose, there is as a rule no certainty as to the die-sequence: in the larger mints it seems probable that there might be several dies, both obverse and reverse, in use at the same time, so that any reverse might go the round of a series of obverses which were standing in the shop; and the process might be repeated with other reverses and the same obverses. The natural result is that, if the die-couplings found in a series of coins from a western mint are arranged in tabular form, numerous crossings are almost certain to appear; and in such a case the order in which the dies were used is much more difficult to determine than for a mint which used fixed dies.

5. At Rome the earliest coins were cast, and the moulds were presumably fitted into one another, so that no variation in the relative positions of the designs on the two faces would occur. When coins began to be struck, the technique of the neighbouring Greek cities influenced the Roman workmen: but by the time of the Empire, only two alternative die-relations are found: the dies are either axially in the same direction or diametrically opposed. The same dual scheme is observable in the issues of some Greek cities in the Imperial period, doubtless due to Roman influence in the mints. As examples may be collected of coins from the same pair of dies, some of which show one and some the other die-position, it seems clear that the dies were so constructed or marked as to ensure that the designs should always be placed in the same plane, though not necessarily the same way up, and that they were not hinged. The method may have been that adopted in some mediaeval Arab dies, in which one of the pair has a peg at either side of the type, and the other has two holes into which the

pegs fit: this makes it possible to place the dies in two positions, but only in these.

6. The length of time during which a die would remain in use would naturally depend to a great extent on the activity of the mint, at any rate in the Greek cities, where the obverse type, the badge of the city, continued unchanged from year to year. In places where the name or badge of the mint-magistrate was put on the coins, the reverse die would have to be altered with a change of magistrates; but this is not likely to have been oftener than once a year in normal circumstances: as already mentioned, an old die which was still serviceable would sometimes be adapted for use under the new magistrate by recutting the name. It is only possible to arrive at any probable conclusion in the series which are definitely dated by an era, or, in the case of the Athenian silver of the third to the first centuries, by months: and these are few in number. At Athens, where the output of coins must have been very large, it has been shown that the normal life of a die did not exceed four months: the mint may be supposed to have been working continuously when the mines were in operation, turning the metal into coin as fast as it was delivered. On the other hand, at Aradus two dies at least are known to have been in use for four successive years: but, as the coins of Aradus seem, following the Athenian precedent, to have been dated by months as well as by years, it also appears that as a rule each shop in the mint

of Aradus only worked for one month in the year: so the result is in effect much the same as at Athens: a die might only serve for four months, but these four months would not be consecutive. In less important cities the occurrence of coins from the same die in successive years may be explained by the small output of the mint: for instance, at Alexandria Troas, where the coins are dated by years, the same die is found in use over a period of four years: but probably few coins were struck at this mint.

7. There is no comparable evidence available as to the life of Roman dies, which have not been studied like the Greek. In regard to one issue of Tiberius, however, it appears probable that the ratio of dies was one obverse to two reverse, which suggests a difference in the handling of the dies in the mint at Rome as compared with those of Greece: this ratio is approximately the same as has been found in respect of English dies of the fourteenth century.

VI. ART

1. A detailed discussion of the artistic styles and schools represented in Greek and Roman coinage would be beyond the scope of these notes; but some general remarks may be found useful.

2. It has been observed that the majority of coins of high artistic quality which were issued during the centuries when Greece dominated the Mediterranean world come from cities of little commercial standing; and, though it would be unsafe to draw a hard and fast line between the artistic and commercial classes of coins in this respect, there is a marked contrast to be noted in the extreme examples of either class. In a city such as Athens, where the first object in striking coins was to make up raw silver from the State's mines in a form convenient for the customers to whom it was to be sold, the chief requirements were exact weight and purity: so long as these were maintained, it mattered little to the buyers, especially in the markets of the Levant, which were importers of Greek silver on a large scale, whether the designs on the coins were of the artistic standard which would be expected by a connoisseur at Athens. Thus, while the boast of Aristophanes, that the tetradrachms of Athens were the only ones correctly struck and refined, was fully justified in fact, it is not easy to agree with

him that they were the most beautiful of all: in his time the designs were archaistic reproductions of those introduced a century earlier. The faithful copying of the old types was due to the same reason which has caused thalers to be struck in the name and with the types of Maria Theresa for more than a century and a half at Vienna and other mints: they had become the recognized currency of Arabia and Abyssinia, and the natives of these countries regarded, and still regard, them as the model coinage. The influence of external markets on style in commercial coinages can be seen in other cases: Aegina, like Athens, was chiefly concerned with the eastern trade, and did not modify the primitive simplicity of its types: Corinth, on the other hand, exported mainly to the west, and Italians and Sicilians were more critical than Phoenicians and Egyptians in artistic matters: so, while the types of the Corinthian coins remained fundamentally the same, their treatment in detail and the execution of the dies show an advance in style comparable to that in other branches of art.

3. On the other hand, cities which did not own or control supplies of silver, and could not therefore determine the price of the metal, would find that one way of securing favour for their coins, and so getting them into circulation, was by making them artistically attractive: a minting authority expects to make a profit on the coins it issues, and if it cannot do this by manipulation of the bullion values, an alternative

course is to turn them into objects of art. The clearest example of a coinage that depended on its artistic merit for its circulation is that of the Eleians, by far the most beautiful of the series of Greece itself. There were probably no mines and no manufactures in Elis in the fifth and fourth centuries, and if there was any export trade it was not considerable—at most some agricultural produce and wood. But every fourth year visitors poured into Elis for the Olympic Games, and brought with them money, which would pass to the officials and the temples and the inhabitants, and leave them at the end of the Games with a glut of silver which they would not be able to get back into circulation in the ordinary course of their business. The most profitable way of dealing with this metal was to turn it into objects which could be sold at a fancy price; and this the Eleians did by striking attractive coins. From a commercial point of view these had no merits, as they were of irregular standard: but as souvenirs of the Games they were just the kind of thing to be popular; and that they succeeded in winning favour is evident from the distribution of the finds that have been recorded. There are several other instances of the issue of long series of artistic coins at cities which were commercially unimportant, particularly in the West: perhaps the most remarkable is that of Terina in South Italy, a city almost unknown to history.

4.   The difference in the degree of attention devoted

to the artistic execution of the coinage at different
cities creates a difficulty in the dating of coins on the
basis of their style: it is as a rule possible to arrive at
a satisfactory arrangement of the issues of a particular
city on this basis, but not to determine which series
were contemporary in two or more cities. In the
Hellenistic and later periods, when there are numerous
sets of dated coins available, it is clear that not only did
the artistic standards of cities which were near neighbours show considerable differences of attainment, but
even in the products of a single mint the level of
execution might vary markedly: it is not infrequently
the case that good and bad dies are used concurrently
for an issue of coins, a good obverse being coupled
with an inferior reverse or vice versa. In most
series the obverses are on the average better than the
reverses, which is not unnatural, in view of the longer
life of the obverse dies: it was not worth while to
spend as much labour on a reverse die as on an obverse which would last several times as long.

5. The most noteworthy instances of good and
bad work being produced together by the same mint
come from Crete, where the coins of some of the
cities definitely suggest that there was a practice of
obtaining a pair of dies executed by a competent
artist, and then having copies of these made by less
skilled hands: that both sets of dies are contemporary
is clear from their joint use. The same method of
multiplication of dies may be traced in some Italian

and Sicilian issues: but, as the copyists there were as a rule fairly skilful, the contrast between the original designs and the reproductions is not so marked as in Crete. Such a variation in the quality of workmanship is of course not surprising, when no mechanical means for the multiplication of dies, such as hubbing from a master die, were available: the use of hubbing may be traced in a certain number of ancient mints, though it has not yet been definitely proved, and in the majority there is no evidence that it was known: in the case of some great recoinages, such as that at Alexandria in the twelfth year of Nero, the endless variety in detail in the dies rules out any suggestion of hubbing.

6. In the Imperial period some outlying provinces of the Roman world produced more or less crude copies of the issues of the mint of Rome, which seem to have been struck officially, and probably represent the local attempts to repeat the types set by the central authorities: there are instances of this in the first century A.D., and it became commoner in the second. There is no reason for regarding these as forgeries made tor private gain: apart from their inferiority of style, they are just as good as the other coins. They thus provide an interesting test of the level of artistic attainment in the provinces where they were struck, in comparison with that of the capital. The economic reason for the issue of these copies was presumably the difficulty of getting supplies of cash from the mint

at Rome: as the control of the central government over the provinces weakened, this difficulty would increase. In the third century the process went further: the 'tyrants' who assumed authority in various parts of the Empire usually established mints of their own, the products of which provide a further index of provincial styles. Finally, Diocletian gave up the attempt to supply the Roman world with coinage from Rome, and a complete decentralization of the system, in art as in other respects, followed.

VII. TYPES

1. The choice of types for Greek and Roman coins becomes more informative for the historian as the coins change their economic character, and pass from mere guaranteed quantities of a commodity into tokens current at artificial values. The earliest types were, as has been mentioned, intrinsically commercial, impressions of the signet of the merchant who had made the metal up in a marketable form, and thus were virtually trademarks. It is as little likely that any personal or historical allusions would be embodied in these signets as in those which are normally used in the East to-day: all that is wanted is a design easily distinguishable from any other that is known in the same district. When the manufacture of coins was taken over by kings and cities, the badge of the king or city was put on the coins in the same way as that of the merchant had been; and when denominations began to be attached to the coins, and a second type on the reverse became of practical service, the field of choice for types was not much extended: the badge of the city might be coupled with the head of a local deity or some familiar object, but in the commercial coinages at any rate the reverse types, when once chosen, did not vary often. The fact that the larger coins, the staters, of these series were used more for

export as bullion than for local trade tended to maintain the importance of the city badge and the city deity as the leading types: it was not till the conquests of Alexander established a uniform currency at fixed values over the eastern part of the Greek world that the predominance of these types was seriously weakened.

2. In Greece itself it is rare to find any direct historical allusion in the types of the coins before Alexander: anything in the nature of portraiture was of course strictly barred by tradition, and equally anything that would tend to identify a particular person as the issuer of a coin. It is true that a custom grew up in certain cities in the fifth century, beginning probably at Corinth, under which the magistrate responsible for the mint placed a distinguishing mark on the coins struck in his period of office: but this was as a rule only a symbol added to the main type, comparable to the earlier signets, or an initial: this would serve to fix the responsibility for the coin for purposes of the state control, but would not convey much to the man in the street. In one or two cities of Northern Greece magistrates' name appear in full, but the formula is, as a rule, that used for datings, and the name is probably that of the eponymous magistrate rather than that of the mint-master. As for political changes, it is sometimes possible to find these reflected in a change of types or fabric, or a modification of those previously used: but in most cases these are of an allusive nature which makes them difficult of

interpretation to the modern student, however full of meaning they may have been to contemporaries. For instance, on the coins of Athens an olive wreath is added to the helmet of Athene about the beginning of the fifth century; but it is quite uncertain whether this refers to the establishment of the democracy or to the victory at Marathon or to that at Salamis, all of which have been suggested, or indeed to something quite different.

3. In the west, however, the types chosen for the coins were from the first more commonly of a suggestive character: there was what might be regarded as an advertising element in the local objects or products portrayed, such as the crab of Acragas or the parsley-leaf of Selinus; or, more markedly, in the head of Dionysos and the bunch of grapes at Sicilian Naxos, where in the sixth century a contingent of vine-growers from the Aegaean Naxos seems to have adopted the coin-types of the mother island with its name in a way that might be regarded as a sort of precedent for Australian Burgundy. This form of advertisement reaches its highest point on the fifth-century coins of Himera, the best-known spa of Sicily, which show a little Satyr standing in a bath under a jet of water flowing from a spout, under the supervision of the local nymph. This tendency developed into the use of types with personal allusions, such as the mule-car on the coins of Rhegium after the victory of the tyrant of Rhegium, Anaxilas, in the races at

Olympia: the most famous example of this class, both in ancient and in modern times, is the Damareteion struck at Syracuse after the defeat of the Carthaginian army at Himera by Gelon, with its crouching lion to symbolize Africa under the victorious quadriga. This was practically a medal, in the modern sense, rather than a coin for currency: it was much larger than any of the coins used in ordinary business, and would probably have been as unpopular for this purpose as a crown piece is to-day: except for the one issue of decadrachms at Athens, which was probably contemporary with it, and may equally be connected with a great victory, nothing of the same kind was produced outside Sicily till the Hellenistic period, and the Sicilian decadrachms seem to be derived from the Damareteion. The tendency to emphasize allusions to important events by pictorial effect is, however, very marked in the designs of the ordinary current coins of Italy and Sicily, as well as on these medallic pieces: it suggests that there was a distinction in the artistic tradition, as applied to coinage, on the east and the west of the Adriatic respectively, which may be compared with that in the religious art of the Greek and Latin churches in later times.

4. The Romans inherited the ideas of the cities of Magna Graecia in this respect: their early bronze coins, it is true, were not Greek in their choice of types, any more than they were in style or fabric: but it was not long after a standard coinage of silver denarii was

started that the types selected became personal and commemorative to a degree that would not have been tolerated in any city of old Greece. The monetary magistrates introduced designs derived from their family legends or their ancestral worships, first on the reverses and then on the obverses of their coins: these gradually became more up to date, in the form of allusions to the exploits of their immediate forefathers, and before the middle of the first century B.C. referred to contemporary events. To make sure that the meaning of the types should be clear to all people, legends were added giving the names of the deities or persons depicted, or brief titles of the particular events commemorated; and under the Empire these legends developed into valuable historical records.

5. The result of this difference of tradition between east and west is that in Greece the coin-types can be used in illustration of history in a certain number of cases, where they can be connected with a fair degree of probability with events known from other sources, but they rarely add any new facts to the evidence derived from literary sources: the history that is to be derived from Greek coins depends far more on the economic information that they convey than on anything of a documentary nature contained in the types and legends. At Rome, on the other hand, the coins are commonly, in and after the first century B.C., direct contemporary evidence, ranking in value with inscriptions for historical purposes. They begin

to lose this character in the third century A.D., and there is little to be learned from them in this respect after the time of Diocletian, except from a few medallions: the ordinary currency shows only constant repetitions of stock types and legends.

6. In connexion with the question of types, however, there is one point to be noted in the Greek series: the borrowing of types by one city from another sometimes gives useful information in regard to political or commercial relations. For instance, the appearance of Rhegian types on the coinage of Zancle-Messana at the beginning of the fifth century would suggest, even if it were not known from other sources, that Zancle had passed into Rhegian control, while the termination of that control is marked by the reappearance of the old Zanclaean types in a single issue, which might be considered to belong to the class of commemorative coins. At Boeotian Orchomenus the old obverse type was a grain of corn, and the city continued to use this when all the other cities of Boeotia struck coins with a common obverse type, the Boeotian shield: at last, in the fourth century, the shield appears on the Orchomenian coins, as a sign that the citizens had abandoned their old attitude of isolation and come into the League. When Abdera began to issue coins, the obverse type adopted was the seated griffin which had been the type of Teos, only differentiated by facing in the opposite directions: the inhabitants of Teos had migrated in a body to Abdera

61

to escape the Persian menace to their liberty, and the choice of this type shows that the refugees regarded themselves as the rightful representatives of the city they had been forced to abandon.

7. The borrowing of types does not however necessarily point to a political connexion, and probably in most cases where it occurs the motives were commercial. Reference has been made already to the use at the Sicilian Naxos of the types of the mother island, and to the advertising implications of this action: also to the importance attached to a type associated with a coinage of good repute in external markets. The most notable instance of the commercial copying of types is in the cases of the Athenian owls: almost immediately after their first issue by Pisistratus, reproductions of them occur, the style of which suggests that they were made at some place or places where the die-engravers were not trained in any of the Greek schools of art; and in the fifth century cruder copies began to appear in the Near East, some probably struck in the interior of Syria and in Nabataea, others, rather later in date, in the Philistine country. Thence they went further afield, and at the end of the fourth century some fairly good coins with types directly derived from the Athenian were produced in Central Asia, while the Syrian copies were recopied in still more debased forms in Mesopotamia and Arabia: the Athenian owl became so thoroughly accepted as the essential type for a coin in Arabia that

it continued to appear till the time of Augustus. But the popularity of Athenian types was not shown in this manner only amongst the barbarians: in the second century B.C. a number of Cretan cities issued staters with the types of the Athenian tetradrachms of the New Style, only varied in the legends and the symbols.

8. Similarly, in the west the commercial influence of Corinth is demonstrated by the spread of the Pegasus type, the constant obverse of the Corinthian coins. Naturally the Corinthian colonies, or rather factories, in the north-west of Greece used the Corinthian types: they were administered from Corinth, and never enjoyed the same independence of the mother city as most Greek colonies. But in the fourth century several cities in the west, not only original Corinthian colonies, such as Syracuse, which had long been self-governing, but places which had no foundational relation with Corinth, such as Locri and Leontini, took to striking with the regular Corinthian types, as if these were the most readily accepted in trade. The influence went further, just as in the case of the types of Athens in the east: the Pegasus appears as an obverse type up the Adriatic in an Illyrian series, and on the east coast of Spain at Emporiae.

9. The popularity of the Athenian and Corinthian types was doubtless due to the fact that the main trade east and west was in the hands of merchants who started from these two cities and took with them to the fringes of the Greek world the coins of their

homes, so that the outsiders would see little else than these in the way of coins. Another kind of commercial connexion can be found in the use of a common type by independent cities, an instance of which is the ox which figures on the obverses of the coins of Byzantium and Chalcedon: the issue of coins with the types of Ephesus at Aradus in the second century points in the same direction, and suggests that there may have been some sort of agreement between the two cities for the common currency of their coinages, which was advertised by the joint use of the types. That such an agreement might have been concluded is shown by the inscription previously mentioned which records an agreement between Mytilene and Phocaea, to provide for the striking of coins on a common standard in alternate years: the inscription is imperfect, but it would presumably proceed to require that the coins of each city should be accepted at the other like its own.

10. A different kind of relationship is indicated by the employment at a city of types which are not native, but are obviously chosen for their connexion with other cities: it is hardly likely that this was intended as a compliment, and a commercial purpose may be suggested. The most remarkable instance of this kind is to be found in the long series of electrum staters of Cyzicus, on which the main types are derived from all round the Aegaean, and the tunny, the badge of Cyzicus, is relegated to a subordinate place. As these

staters formed a sort of international currency, and occur in hoards in all parts of Greece, it seems most probable that supplies may have been produced at Cyzicus on the order of foreign clients and stamped with types appropriate to the tastes of those clients. It is also not improbable that the so-called island coins of the sixth century, silver staters of Aeginetan weight and fabric, but with badges which in most cases belong to sundry of the Aegaean islands, were actually struck at a central mint at Aegina for these islands.

11. The choice of types with a complimentary purpose does occur in Greek cities, but not before the Imperial period: then a number of places in Asia Minor struck coins with types commemorating the 'Homonoia' of two or more cities, usually the chief deities greeting one another: but this can hardly be interpreted as referring to any commercial understanding, in view of the limited degree of control of trade granted to the Greek cities by the Roman Empire.

12. The earliest coinage in the name of the Romans provides some examples of the borrowing of types which may fairly be called commercial in origin, though the actual occasion was military. At the beginning of the third century B.C. a silver coinage was issued which in standard, style, and types corresponded closely to the staters of the Greek cities of South Italy, but bore the legend ROMANO or later ROMA. The types were derived from several

65

sources: one is a close copy of an obverse type of
Metapontum, another a free imitation of the horse's
head which was a frequent reverse on the Carthaginian
coinage for Sicily, others are definitely Campanian.
As there were Roman armies in the field in South
Italy at this period, who would need to obtain supplies
from the Greek cities, many of which were their
allies and so would have to be paid for their goods,
it was only natural that the Roman commanders, at a
period when there was no coinage struck at Rome,
should have coins made locally which would corres-
pond in all essentials to those in normal circulation in
the districts where they were operating. The same
need produced a similar coinage later, when Sulla,
during his campaign in Greece, struck tetradrachms of
the standard Athenian types, but with his badge instead of the name of Athens. Such an occasion would
not of course recur under the Empire, when the
Roman coinage had become a world-currency.

VIII. MINTS

1. There is no definite evidence that a mint, as a regularly organized part of the state machinery, existed at any city in Greece except Athens: magistrates were chosen to be responsible for coinage, but it does not appear through what course of action they fulfilled their responsibility. Even at Athens the information is vague: there was an establishment where, from its name, it may be concluded that silver was struck, and there are references to keeping standards: but it does not appear whether it was under direct or indirect State control. At the majority of the cities which issued coins in the Greek world, as will be seen later, the output must have been so spasmodic that it would hardly have been worth while to maintain a regular staff for minting purposes: the needs of currency could have been adequately met by commissioning local silversmiths to strike coins. The control of the State could have been exercised, much as it was in England in the early Middle Ages, by issuing official dies to the moneyers and testing their products. An alternative method, which there is reason to think was adopted in some cases, would be to send an order to another city which was better equipped for the work: so the London Mint now strikes coins for many foreign countries.

67

2. The evidence which has already been collected with regard to the restriking of coins shows that in many cities there would be no need for any machinery more elaborate than a pair of dies: all else could be provided in the ordinary apparatus of the smith. Only at the chief silver-marketing centres, such as Aegina, Corinth, and Athens, would there be shops for smelting, refining, and casting the blanks: and some part of this may have been done elsewhere, at the mines. The degree of responsibility placed on the persons appointed to supervise the coinage would therefore vary from place to place; but as a rule it would probably be concerned only with the purity of the metal, as indicated by the Mytilene-Phocaea agreement.

3. This agreement suggests that at Mytilene and Phocaea there was only one man at a time in office; and the names of magistrates which appear in many other places would be consistent with this. At more important centres it would be natural to have a larger board: so at Athens in the second century B.C. two or three names occur together on an issue of coins, and there are indications that similar groupings existed elsewhere: at Rome under the Republic there were three monetary magistrates in office annually. But it is not known how they shared their responsibilities: there is some evidence that more than one shop might be operating at a city, but the relation of the shops to the officials has not been traced. It is not till the

Imperial period, when the mints were, like modern mints, organized as a regular part of the Civil Service, that the system of shopmarks can be definitely discovered.

4.   There is just as little definite evidence concerning the output of any Greek or Roman mint: no ancient author has preserved details of the amount of bullion converted into coin at any time or place, and the information that may be deduced from the coins that have survived is speculative to a high degree.   It may be taken as certain that the coins now known to us are a very small proportion of those that were originally struck: the frequency with which 'unpublished' types are described suggests this conclusion: for example, the Alexandrian series has been as carefully examined as any, and over ten thousand varieties have been recorded, but any large hoard from Egypt is almost sure to contain some further additions to the list.   In the case of any series of which a Corpus has been published, it can be seen that many varieties are known from single specimens only, and, except in those instances where a type was struck without modification over a period of years, it is quite usual for not more than four or five specimens to be recorded, especially in the minor Greek mints.   As it can be shown that in certain mediaeval coinages, where details of the output have been preserved in the mint records, the number of specimens now surviving is probably about one in five thousand of those struck, it is not unreasonable to

assume that ancient coinages may have suffered a like fate: if this is correct, there is an even chance that any issue which did not exceed five thousand pieces may have vanished off the face of the earth.

5. Some idea of the comparative quantities of currency issued at different times and places may, however, be derived from a study of recorded facts, more particularly as to the finds; and this is useful for the economic side of history. The issues of a mint doubtless varied according to the demand in ancient times, as they do to-day: if there are enough pennies in circulation, the London Mint will let a year or two pass without striking any more; and the average Greek city would be just as unlikely to produce coins that were not wanted. The great silver-marketing cities, such as Athens and Corinth, might turn their raw metal into staters as it came in, because these were largely put on the market as bullion for export, not for local circulation: but in the normal circumstances of a Greek city which did not control silver-mines there would be no point in continuously striking coins. Some idea of the way in which the activities of a Greek mint might be governed by seasonal demands may be obtained from the issues of Aradus, where the staters were regularly dated not only by the year but by the month of issue, if the most probable explanation of the mint-letters is accepted: in a period of ninety-two years, eighty-two dates are known, and of these all but seven are in the first or last, the fourth or fifth,

or the eighth month of the years; it may be surmised that these were the months in which the caravans set out for the interior country. The degree of annual variation in the coinage of Alexandria under the Roman Empire can be determined with some approach to probability: enormous numbers of Alexandrian tetradrachms have been found in Egypt in recent years—a single collector stated that he had had over a million through his hands—and, as these tetradrachms were always dated by the regnal years of the emperors, a useful table of the comparative numbers for each year can be obtained. It appears that no coins whatever are known for some few years, and in others nothing was struck except fractional bronze pieces. The standard coin for trade purposes was the debased silver tetradrachm, and both the total numbers of specimens recorded and the comparative numbers from consecutive years found in hoards show clearly that the output went up and down irregularly: no political reasons for these variations can be traced, so it is fair to conclude that the considerations that governed them were commercial.

6. It should be noted here that some care must be exercised in laying stress on the content of a hoard for the purpose of determining the size of an issue, and still more on the mere number of specimens recorded as known: in the case of the Alexandrian series the risk is not so great as in some, since the evidence is cumulative, derived from a large number of hoards;

but there are many instances of a type or variety which was accounted rare becoming common, in the collector's sense of the word, after a large hoard has been found and dispersed. This will be more fully discussed in the section dealing with the meaning of hoards.

7. Another way in which some useful statistics as to the size of issues can be obtained, at any rate for purposes of comparison, is from the numbers of different dies which are known to have been employed: this will not show the actual size of a particular issue, since the number of coins which could be struck from an ancient Greek or Roman die has not been determined. The largest number of specimens from a single pair of dies which has been recorded is 334, in a find of gold coins of the fifth century A.D. from the Forum at Rome: it may be surmised that the person who collected the hoard had drawn a supply of solidi from a bank just after they had come in from the mint, and hidden his money forthwith: but there is no likelihood that his parcel comprised the whole output of this pair of dies. But it may be assumed that the dies in use at any given mint would have about the same life on the average, measuring life by the number of coins struck from the dies; so, if, in a series where the coins are dated, several dies are found in use in one year, while in another year only one die is known, it is fairly safe to conclude that in the former year the mint was busier than in the latter. In important mints a great many

dies might be used in a single year: at Alexandria, when the issue of silver tetradrachms was resumed after a lapse of fifty years in the seventh year of Tiberius, a calculation has shown that probably 610 obverse dies were used; but this was a rather exceptional issue, though not the largest on record from this mint. On the other hand, it is not uncommon to find a single obverse die used by three different magistrates in succession, in mints where the practice of having fixed dies was the rule: this means that at any rate the middle magistrate of the three was not responsible for so large an issue as to wear out one obverse die. But at the same mints instances may be found of the use of two or three obverse dies by the same magistrate: this is an additional proof of the irregularity of output.

8. Unless, however, some fresh source of information can be discovered, our estimates of the sizes of particular issues can only be comparative. In the later periods of Greek coinage, and in Roman coinage generally, as an issue can usually be delimited in point of time by names or symbols of magistrates, if not by actual dates, this comparison is economically instructive: but in the earlier Greek series, where a type might be kept in service for many years without modification and without any symbols or names, it is hardly ever possible to date coins with the degree of precision necessary for comparing the size of issues. The great irregularity which has been shown to have occurred

in the dated issues, alike in size and in continuity, makes more pronounced the danger of trying to draw any systematic conclusions from those which have not the clue given by dates.

IX. COUNTERMARKS

1. Countermarking a coin—that is to say, impressing a secondary stamp upon it—is as a rule done either in order to give a fresh guarantee to the coin by a new authority, or to vary the value placed on it when it was originally issued by the same authority which countermarked it. In the former case, the process of countermarking practically served the same end as that of restriking a coin, which has already been described, and only differed from it in the degree of thoroughness with which the first designs were obliterated. If the mint-masters of a city desired to re-use coins and to mark them for the purpose of circulation in their city, but could not provide dies which would cover the whole face of the coins, the result would be that the coins would appear with a rim of the original design round the countermark on either side. Such imperfect restriking, as it really was, is not found in the cities of Greece, which were generally more thorough in their work: but it occurs not infrequently in the issues of several cities of Asia Minor in the Hellenistic period, usually in the bronze series, but occasionally in the silver: in the latter case the coins countermarked were not foreign ones, but pieces of an earlier series of the city itself, which were

75

stamped with types derived from those of a later series. The reason for countermarking in these cases is not clear: the coins so treated are not as a rule worn, and, if it was intended to give a new denomination to them, there is nothing to show what that was, though this may have been made known at the time by proclamation: a proclamation relating to the acceptance of currency is recorded by Aristophanes. It is possible that for some reason or other the first issuers of the coins had fallen into disfavour, and their successors wished, without going to the trouble of calling in the coins, to restore their credit by showing that they were still approved by the body responsible for the currency of the city: but our knowledge of the history of the cities concerned does not enable us to test the validity of this suggestion in any instance.

2. Countermarking for the purpose of revaluation was more frequent in the Imperial period in the Greek series of Asia, especially in the third century A.D., when monetary values were dropping rapidly throughout the Empire, and the bronze coinages of the cities, which were still the chief local currency for low denominations, had to be brought into relation with the depreciating denarius: the usual method adopted was to stamp the coin with a figure showing the number of assaria for which it was to be accepted. These countermarked pieces can be used to provide a commentary on the economic situation in the districts in which they occur.

3. On the Roman bronze of the early Empire there is a good deal of countermarking with a stamp of a few letters giving the name of an Emperor in an abbreviated form: it occurs most frequently with the names of Tiberius and Nero. The purpose of this seems to have been to signify the approval by a new Emperor of the coins of his predecessors: there is no ground for thinking that the coinage was revalued, and the original types of the counterstamped pieces are often perfectly clear, so that there was no obvious need of a fresh guarantee to secure their acceptance: it may be that the people had not got used to the idea of a continuing Imperial authority, and it was thought desirable to emphasize the confirmation by a new Emperor of the acts of his predecessor. The instances where coins issued with the portrait of one Emperor were counterstamped with that of his successor, which chiefly occur in the provinces, are probably to be ascribed to local zeal rather than to any definite policy dictated by the government: even in cases of the damnatio memoriae of an Emperor, the erasure of his likeness or titles on coins, like the erasures on inscriptions, was only sporadic.

4. In some series of Greek coins there are numerous instances of the impression of small punchmarks, less conspicuous than the ordinary kind of countermarks, which appear to have served a somewhat different purpose from these. As a rule they do not show any type

more elaborate than a slight geometric ornament, and often are no more than mere holes or scratches: there are only a few instances of the kind of type that would be recognizable as a city badge, or of any lettering. The earliest examples of this class are to be found on the electrum coins of the Lydian kings in the seventh century: they are common on the coins of the Eleians in the fifth century, on those issued at Aegina before the capture of the island by the Athenians in the middle of the same century, and on the silver sigloi of the kings of Persia: the most extensive use of such marks is in Egypt in the early years of Ptolemaic rule. The probable explanation of these punchmarks is that they were impressed by silver-merchants or others who circulated the coins as bullion, or at any rate at bullion values, not at the values in specie assigned to them by their issuers: it is consistent with this theory that the marks on some staters of Alexander found in Egypt can be read as Aramaic names or formulae. The Lydian coins were probably the first to which a value in specie had ever been attached, and the Greek merchants who handled them would hardly be likely to recognize the artificial valuation of the kings. The coins of the Eleians were, as suggested already, medals or objects of art in the estimation of their producers, which might be sold at a fancy price at Olympia; but if the purchaser took them away and wished to realize, he would only get their bullion value, unless he could

78

dispose of them to a collector of such objects. The guarantee for the coins of Aegina ceased with the Athenian conquest, as that for the Persian sigloi after the fall of the kingdom, and consequently they would, in modern terms, no longer be quoted in the exchange markets of Greece. The silver currency introduced into Egypt by Alexander had a nominal value based on the Greek price of silver, which could only hold good in Egypt so long as that country was part of the Alexandrine Empire: as soon as the Empire broke up, and Egypt became a kingdom by itself, the local price of silver, which was much higher than in Greece, came into play, and the face-values of the coins were far below their bullion values. In all these cases, therefore, there were practical reasons for the demonetization of the coins; and this was signified for trade purposes by the punchmarks impressed on them. The denomination of a Greek coin was of course valid only in the territory of its home state, unless a reciprocal agreement for the acceptance of currency had been made between two or more cities—such may have existed in many more cases than those of which records have been preserved. But, so long as a city's credit was good, there would be no great difficulty in negotiating the acceptance of its coins by bankers in foreign countries: Rhodian drachmas were in fact accepted in Tenos at a premium of about five per cent, though the average weight of the Rhodian drachma is slightly less than that of the Tenian. The punchmarking of a coin virtually signified that the bankers would not quote an exchange rate for it, and converted it into an ingot.

X. STANDARDS

1. The coinage standards of European Greece, in the period of city autonomy, were all dependent on the three great silver markets, Aegina, Corinth, and Athens: each of these had its own standard drachma, and the weight of the drachma at other cities was practically determined by their connexion with one or other of the three. If a city was in the Aeginetan commercial circle, it would use the Aeginetan coins that came to it in the course of trade; and, when it desired to issue a coinage of its own, would restrike these coins. As the coins, on the average, would have lost weight by wear and tear, the result would be that the average weight of the drachma of the city which did the restriking would be somewhat less than the Aeginetan, and, so far as that city could be said to have a standard, it would be what is sometimes called a reduced Aeginetan one. Nearly all the minor variants of standard found in the Greek world, exclusive of Asia and some outlying districts, can be explained in this way.

2. The Aeginetan standard seems to have been the invention of Pheidon of Argos, who took in hand the regulation of the currency of the Peloponnesus: before his time the unit of value had been the drachma, which was not a coin, but was represented for purposes of

measuring prices by a bundle of iron rods, which were virtually counters. The Aeginetan merchants had coined their silver into ingots of a size convenient for handling, the weights of which were rather irregular, possibly not intended to conform to a standard: Pheidon attributed to these a fixed value in terms of the old unit, the drachma, which would hold good regardless of fluctuations in the price of silver as metal. The Aeginetan ingot weighed on the average about 185 grains, and after Pheidon's reform it was called a didrachm; this was presumably the nearest round figure to its bullion value, after a deduction had been made for safety against loss: the result was that the Aeginetan standard drachma had a weight of slightly over ninety grains.

3. The first alternative standard that appeared in Greece was the Corinthian: the authorities at Corinth, seeing that the Aeginetan ingot was accepted in trade as representing two drachmas, although it might be worth less as metal, followed Pheidon's lead and issued a coinage of their own on an independent standard. This was based on an ingot which weighed about 130 grains, which is so near the weight of the Babylonian commercial shekel that it may be assumed to have been derived from it. The Corinthians gave this stater the nominal value of three drachmas, which meant a drachma of less than half the weight of the Aeginetan.

4. The commercial weight system from which

this ingot was derived was used in Euboea and Attica as well as in Corinth, and was probably an import from Ionia: it does not appear that it included the drachma as a weight, and, if the ingot had any specific description, it would presumably be reckoned as a sixtieth of a mina. Since the drachma was a term of value only, it was open to any city to assign to the ingot a denomination of any number of drachmas that suited its market: so the Euboean cities before the end of the seventh century struck staters of the same weight as the Corinthian, which they called didrachms. This standard was adopted by Solon in his reform programme for Athens, and with a slight modification it became the Athenian standard.

5. The most important innovation of Solon in this connexion was that he made weights related to his coinage: that is, he created a commercial weight and gave it the name of the old term of value, the drachma, fixing it at one-hundredth of the mina: his coinage was based on this, with an allowance or agio of five per cent to cover the costs of the mint, so that he struck 6,300 drachma coins out of 6,000 commercial drachmas weight of silver. The relationship of the two systems was not unlike that of the avoirdupois and Troy scales in the English system, except that the English start at the bottom with a common grain, the Greek at the top with a common talent.

6. All the coinage standards of European Greece are modifications of these three; in some outlying

regions, notably in Thrace before the fifth century, there are series which do not fall in with any one of them; but in these cases the explanation must be that there was in reality no standard at all in the Greek sense. The coins of the tribes were not valued by them in terms of Greek currency, but were simply ingots of sizes determined by convenience for trade: when a mining community had a regular customer, it would naturally tend to make up its silver in ingots suited to the demands of its clients, but the market might vary from time to time; and similarly the weights varied.

7. In the western area of Greek trade, which was mainly exploited by the Corinthians and the Euboeans, the Greek colonies for the most part used the stater which was common to the two sets of merchants: but the divisions of it had to be modified to suit the local measures of value. In Sicily the native tribes of the interior used copper or bronze as their standard metal, and their unit was the litra, which was divided into twelfths: in order to facilitate exchange, the Greek cities struck small coins of silver which were equivalent to the litra of bronze at current market rates, with the result that the silver litra varied in weight considerably at different centres, and could seldom be treated as a simple fraction of the stater. A further complication was introduced into the standards of the cities of the west of Sicily by the fact that an independent—that is, not Greek-controlled—supply of silver came into the

market from Spain, in the seventh and early sixth centuries probably in Greek ships, but later through Carthage, which led to a slight raising of the standard of weight at these cities as the result of the competition. In Italy the modifications were less marked, partly because the tribes of Central Italy do not seem to have accepted silver as a measure of exchange to the same extent as the Sicels and Elymians, partly because the Etruscans were not such serious competitors in the metal markets of South Italy as the Carthaginians were in those of Sicily.

8. The coinage standards of Asia Minor and the adjacent islands were similarly affected by local considerations. For a century after the introduction of the Aeginetan standard in Greece, it dominated the Aegaean markets south of Chios: but those to the north seem to have begun to derive their supply of silver direct from Thrace as early as 600, and to have developed a standard of their own to suit their prices: this spread southwards, till by the end of the fifth century it was so firmly established at Rhodes that it is commonly known as the Rhodian standard. The fifth century standards of Chios and Phocaea are heavier than the Rhodian, presumably because the cost of transport from Thrace was less there than to Rhodes; and there is a gradual drop along the line southwards. But on the mainland the cities had to deal with markets accustomed to the Persian standard, which, for silver, was an artificial one: the Persian

coinage was based on a gold unit, the daric of about 130 grains, and silver was struck at a fixed ratio of $13\frac{1}{3}$: 1, which gave a silver siglos of about eighty grains as the twentieth of the daric. This was midway between the Aeginetan and the Athenian drachmas in weight, and seems to have been current as a drachma in retail trade in the Greek cities of the west coast: and those of them to which the trade with the interior was more important than that overseas, such as Colophon, struck their coinage on the Persian standard. The effects on local coinage of the re-use of old coins are very clearly shown in this connexion: when the Persian silver was demonetized and thrown on the market after the fall of the Persian Empire, a number of cities on the west coast issued coins apparently on the Persian standard, sometimes concurrently with others on the Rhodian, which can best be explained as restruck Persian sigloi.

9. Another local standard is found in Phoenicia: the first coinage used here was Persian, but, as Greek influence grew in the fifth century, and Greek silver, mainly Athenian, competed with the Persian, a coinage developed which was in effect a Greek one on a standard somewhat lower than the Athenian. The reduction was presumably due to costs of transport, and in accordance with this the standard was lower in the southern cities of Phoenicia, Tyre and Sidon, than in the north at Aradus: a further drop appears in the coins struck in Philistia and later in North Arabia.

10. The only part of the African coast where there is any question of coin-standards is in Cyrenaica: and here no local standard seems to have existed at any time. Probably all the Cyrenaic coins were restruck on coins imported from abroad—many of the earlier certainly were—and it seems to have been a matter of indifference whether these were on the Athenian or the Asiatic standard.

11. All local Greek standards, east of the Adriatic, were temporarily swept away by the establishment of a uniform coinage under Alexander: this was based on the Athenian silver unit, supplemented by gold at a fixed ratio for higher denominations, and the same rates of value were stabilized throughout the Empire. But as soon as the Empire broke up, the common standard collapsed: the Alexandrine system continued in the kingdoms of Macedonia and Syria, supplemented by the Athenian, with which it was practically identical, till the middle of the second century, because it was based on Greek values: but where the local price of silver was higher, as in Phoenicia and Egypt, the coinage standard was adapted to this almost at once. The Egyptian coinage was reduced to the Phoenician basis before 300, and the Ptolemies continued to coin on this standard in their possessions on the Phoenician and Syrian coasts throughout the third century: when the Seleucids took their place, though there was a temporary break in the issues of silver shekels from the Phoenician mints, by the middle of

the second century the kings were striking special coins on the Phoenician standard concurrently with those of the Alexandrine standard produced at the central mint of Antioch, and before the end of the century several of the more important cities were striking in their own names and on their own standards. During this period the kings of Egypt, who no longer needed to consider the wishes of the merchants of Phoenicia, as they had done when they were responsible for providing them with currency, had reduced the standard of their silver coinage to suit the Egyptian market, where the price of silver was abnormally high; and in the first century the Egyptian tetradrachm contained only a quarter of the silver that an Athenian did.

12. The rise of the power of Rome, however, stopped the development of local standards in the Greek East, and led to the use of a uniform currency over a wider area and for a longer period than that of Alexander. Initially the Roman coinage was on a bronze standard, as was natural in Italy: when the tribes of central Italy, who had used rough lumps of cast bronze for purposes of trade, began to fashion them more after the Greek model with definite types to show their origin, the coins were made on the standard of the Italian libra, and were of the full weight of the metal: they bore no mark of denomination, and presumably passed at their metal value. But the Etruscans had, as early as the fifth century, followed Greek precedent by striking gold and silver with

88

marks of value, and probably about 400 did the same with their bronze: this resulted in a gradual drop in the weight of the coins, as nearly always occurs in a coinage rated at a value in specie. The Italian tribes followed suit, and, whereas the early coinages without marks of value are usually of good weight, as soon as such marks are introduced the weights drop. Rome was one of the last of the Italian communities to start a coinage, and when it did so, the idea of denominations had taken firm root in Italy: the first Roman bronze asses are considerably below a libra in weight, and their weight dropped rapidly under the stress of the Punic wars, till they had no more than a nominal value.

13. Not long after the inception of the bronze coinage at Rome the development of trade with the Greek cities had brought home to the authorities the need of a silver coinage for purposes of dealing with the merchants who were accustomed to think in terms of silver; and two series of silver coins were started, the quadrigatus, approximately the weight of the Campanian didrachm, and the victoriatus, approximately that of the Illyrian drachma: these had a metal ratio to the bronze libra of about 120:1, the normal Greek ratio of the time. In the middle of the second Punic war the Roman authorities decided to abandon the attempt to keep bronze as their standard of coinage, and to express the value of the bronze unit in silver: since the price of bronze had risen to a very high figure,

they took a ratio of 20:1, known as the sextantal standard, and struck a denarius with the fixed value of ten asses, approximately three-fifths of the weight of the quadrigatus, the exchange value of which had been quoted at sixteen asses. The produce of the State mines, especially those in Spain, enabled the Romans to control the price of silver, and so to stabilize the currency, more effectually than they could have done with a bronze standard. Thereafter the denarius continued as the virtual unit of the Roman coinage throughout the period of the Empire: gold and bronze coins were added to the series for higher and lower values, but related to the denarius for their denominations; and the silver content of the denarius remained almost stable, except for a slight drop under Nero, till the collapse of the central power in the third century. The denarius then begun to depreciate, and the history of the Roman currency till the end of the Western Empire shows no trace of any fixed standard, only a succession of attempts to produce a token coinage which would maintain its nominal value, all of which failed. When Anastasius took in hand the reorganization of the coinage of the Eastern Empire to provide a world currency, he frankly abandoned the denarius and started afresh on a gold standard.

XI. HOARDS

1. A hoard of coins, in the strictest sense of the term, is an assemblage of currency which has been deposited purposely in a place of concealment or safety; but in common usage, since it is often difficult to determine whether coins that have been found together were intentionally hidden or lost by accident, any such coins which appear to have been hidden or lost as a group are regarded as a hoard. The meaning of a hoard for the purpose of historical evidence is affected to some extent by the circumstances of its deposit or loss, if these can be ascertained; but in any case it will fall into a different class from that of coins scattered sporadically or found singly about a spot inhabited or frequented at any period. Finds of coins may therefore be treated under the two heads of hoards and casual finds.

2. Many hoards come into the market without any details of the place or surroundings in which they were found, and consequently lose much of their historical value: it is sometimes possible to secure information on these points by a process of detective investigation, but this information is apt to be coloured, if the finder thinks that it is in his own interest to keep the truth a secret, or that he can enhance the market price of his coins by the story which he tells; and, unless

independent corroboration is available, details so obtained should usually be accepted with reserve. Even if the information is honestly given, it is apt to be vague and unscientific: it is not sufficient to learn that a hoard was found under the floor or in the wall of a house, without further particulars which might show whether the find-spot was a regular place of deposit, used possibly over a considerable period, or a temporary hide, or even what might be called accidental, due to the collapse of the house or some similar event. In such a case details of stratification, of the kind given by scientific excavators, are essential, and these are not likely to be noted by the ordinary man. The meaning of a hoard said to have been found in a pot in a field or to have been thrown up in digging is even more hard to assess: here not only are the immediate surroundings important, but it should be ascertained whether any buildings or roads are known to have existed in the vicinity, as this might help to determine whether the hoard was purposely concealed or was simply a casual loss.

3. The majority of hoards can be grouped in two classes, as domestic or as mercantile hoards: official hoards and robbers' hoards are less frequently found. As will be seen, the composition of a hoard is not in itself a sufficient indication of the class to which it belongs: other evidence, if available, must be taken into account before the interpretation of a hoard is attempted, since two hoards of similar composition

may have quite distinct historical values if they were secreted under different circumstances; and it is because such evidence is so rarely obtainable that the use of hoards as historical material has been regarded with suspicion in many quarters.

4. The typical domestic hoard is really of the same character as the proverbial stocking, which has been replaced to a very large extent by the savings bank: spare cash is hidden in some place of safety in or near the owner's house, such as a hole in the wall or above a beam or under the floor: it is rare for the hide to be outside the house, but this does sometimes occur. A hoard of this nature is normally composed of the best coins in circulation: if there has been a depreciation of the currency, the hoarder naturally chooses the older coins to put away, in accordance with the principle underlying Gresham's law; and there is an equally natural tendency to take the largest denominations readily available—thus a Greek hoard will usually have a preponderance of staters, a Roman of denarii. This tendency may be seen in the composition of English hoards, which rise from pennies to groats after the Plantagenets, under the Stuarts are mainly of shillings and half-crowns, and were beginning to show a preference for gold when the development of banks did away with the need for hoarding amongst the wealthier classes. The same desire to save the best coins at hand is often traceable in an evident preference for pieces in good condition in the formation of a

hoard: the proportion of badly-worn coins in a Greek or Roman domestic hoard is usually much smaller than that in the casual finds which presumably represent the ordinary currency of the time. From this indication it is sometimes possible to trace the accumulation of a hoard over a considerable period, especially where the currency was composed of dated coins, as was the case in Egypt under the Roman Empire: several hoards have been recorded in which the earlier coins are all more or less worn, but at a point in the series most of the pieces begin to be in fresh condition, and this may continue the case for several years: the conclusion may be drawn that this point indicates the time when the collector of the hoard started his work, afterwards adding from year to year the newest coins that he could. Such a hoard would probably be accumulated only when economic conditions were fairly stable, and there was a steady supply of fresh coinage coming into circulation: it would hardly be possible at a time of stress, such as the fifth century A.D., when most of the mints of the Roman world were in a state of collapse, and the provincials had to manage as best they could with any old coins that had survived.

5. Mercantile hoards are more varied than domestic in their character and composition, since the purposes for which they might be wanted could be of many kinds. The object of the domestic hoard is usually much the same in the end, to collect a reserve of cash; but the merchant might intend to use his coins

as capital, or as change for convenience in trade, or as bullion, to give some common examples; and in each of these cases the composition of the hoard would tend to differ. In the earliest period of the use by the Greeks of coined metal, it was essentially a commodity which passed from hand to hand at its bullion value: the hoards of this period are frequently composed of pieces belonging to different currencies, sometimes mixed up with a quantity of scrap metal, which clearly indicates that the first consideration in the mind of the merchant would be the quality of the metal, and the denomination which might have been given to any coin by its issuer would not determine its price in his market. Naturally in such a hoard, if it was formed on any regular line of trade, the coinage of the starting-point of the line would predominate, but other coinages, if they were of good repute, would not be excluded: it is instructive to note how in Egypt and Syria some issues were normally cut across, as a test to make sure they were not plated, whilst others were accepted without any such test.

6. After the early years of the fifth century B.C. the conditions of inter-state trade became more stabilized, and regular rates of exchange were formulated; and, partly as a result of this, mixed hoards are less frequently found dating from this period in the Greek world. For his own convenience a merchant would prefer to handle currencies of one and the same standard, and this would make the currency of each line of

traffic more homogeneous: also, because the value of a coin in specie is normally higher than as bullion, any external currency that reached a city would find its best market with the money-changers or with merchants who could repatriate it: there would be no advantage, rather the reverse, in hoarding it. The typical mercantile hoard of the fifth or fourth century B.C. is composed predominantly of the issues of the state in which it was formed; and, if there are any external coins, they are usually of neighbouring cities: also there is not the same preference for staters as in the domestic hoard, since any denomination might be equally useful in retail trade. Where mixed hoards do occur, it may be surmised that they are the stores of money-changers or bankers: the kind of collection of miscellaneous currency that might be accumulated in such a case can be seen from such documents as the accounts of the treasurers of the temple of Delos, where the coins are classified under several heads according to their standards. Occasionally the contents of a hoard of this kind may suggest the circumstances which led to its formation: a lot of small coins with a marked proportion of worn pieces amongst them may be surmised to be the contents of the till of a shopkeeper, while a collection of freshly struck pieces may represent the cash drawn for a purchasing expedition; but this cannot be more than conjectural, unless some details as to the circumstances in which the hoard was found are recorded and give additional light.

For instance, a hoard entirely made up of copper pentadrachms, the smallest denomination in currency, was unearthed in the precincts of a temple in Egypt: as the pentadrachm was used for setting in action an automatic machine for the supply of lustral water at the entrance of Egyptian temples, it is not improbable that this hoard represents the takings of such a machine.

7. So far as Roman coins are concerned, it is more difficult to distinguish between the different types of hoards on the evidence of their contents: after the middle of the second century B.C. the currency of Rome consisted mainly of denarii, and all hoards were alike; whilst under the Empire there was only the one world currency in the West, which spread gradually to the East, till the last independent provincial issues ended with the monetary reform of Diocletian. It is rare to find in the composition of a hoard of the Imperial period any clue as to the purposes for which it was collected, though occasionally something may be learned from the conditions in which it was discovered.

8. Official hoards are rarely found: in Greece they seem to be unknown before the Hellenistic period, proabably because the ordinary Greek city or community had no reserve of cash to put away: some of the temples were wealthy, but they would not need to secrete their coins. A few Hellenistic hoards, such as the Demanhur hoard of Alexandrine tetradrachms, may be of the nature of military chests, and there

are several examples of the same kind from Roman times: these are normally homogeneous and composed mainly of coins in unworn condition, but they are not likely to be informative for the purposes of history in respect of their contents, though if there is any clue to the circumstances of their deposit they may throw some light on military movements.

9. Robbers' hoards are occasionally interesting, though here the conditions of discovery are particularly important: a quantity of treasure buried to save it from the risk of theft might well be composed of the same kinds of property as the proceeds of a raid; but in most cases the former would be put away within easy reach of the owner's house, while the latter would be secreted in some out-of-the-way spot. A few hoards, however, are recorded in which ornaments, coins, and other objects of value were stacked together in confusion, as if they were a mere collection of scrap metal, and these may almost certainly be regarded as loot. Here the composition of the hoard may prove instructive, as the objects in it may give some hints as to the sources from which they came and so to the movements of the robbers. Historically hoards of this class are important in the later years of the Roman Empire, when raids of barbarians on the frontiers were frequent events, on account of the information that they may convey about such raids: in earlier times they do not suggest much beyond a breakdown in the police arrangements of the districts in which they occur.

Economically they are even less valuable; but they do provide material for the student of social conditions.

10. Casual finds are really much more useful for history than hoards, if treated with due discrimination; but there are several points in regard to which caution must be exercised. In the first place, it must be remembered that the finding of a single coin in itself has little or no value as historical evidence: for instance, the attempts to prove the continuance of the occupation of certain districts by the Romans after the dates usually accepted for their withdrawal, on the ground that one or two Roman coins of later dates have been found there, are really baseless: stray coins drift anywhere at all periods, and may be dropped long after their issue. It is only when the circumstances of their deposit can be ascertained, as for instance in a grave, that such finds are likely to provide useful evidence. But if in a given area coins are found in some numbers, singly or otherwise, the strength of their testimony grows in a geometrical progression as the numbers increase; and if the list of coins of the same issue or class reaches double figures, there is a fair probability that they represent the ordinary currency of that district about the time when they were struck. Such finds need to be tabulated with some care: it must be noted in this connexion, that a hoard, of whatever size, only counts as a unit in the table: properly treated, however, they can furnish important historical evidence.

11. For economic purposes it is necessary also to consider how the coins may have reached the spot where they were found: this may be illustrated from the records of Roman finds in England. The majority of these of course belong to the period of the Roman occupation, and offer no difficulty; but there are fairly numerous instances of what may be called intrusions, such as Greek bronze of the third to first centuries B.C., which may have come over in various ways. It is unlikely that any of them would be brought by traders before the first century B.C., unless they were dropped accidentally by a foreigner who was visiting the country: they would certainly have no value, except as curiosities, to the Britons. It is more probable that they came with the Roman soldiers: a clear case of this kind appears in the votive deposit at Procolitia on the wall of Hadrian, where at least three Greek coins were found amongst some thousands of Roman in the well at which the deity Coventina was invoked. There is no reason to think that the deposit of coins in the well began before the district was occupied by the Romans, as there are no traces of any earlier visitors: so these Greek coins must have been brought up two or three centuries after their issue by the soldiers, possibly as keepsakes or amulets, and dropped into the well. A similar explanation may be given for a good many finds of coins far from their homes and from any region in which they can ever have been current: the fact that they are often pierced

for suspension supports this theory. But after the establishment of the Roman Empire, the proportion of intrusive coins that can be attributed to backwaters of traffic increases: bronze coins issued by Greek cities of the Eastern provinces in the first to third centuries A.D. turn up on Romano-British sites in the South of England, especially near the coast: such coins would not be likely to be acceptable to the Britons, unless they bore a fairly close resemblance to the Imperial coinage; but if they were offered to the natives by sailors or travellers who had come from the East they would probably be thrown away—very much in the same manner as modern European currency gets scattered over most parts of England at the present time.

12. Such casual finds are important, as they imply some direct connexion, probably either of a mercantile or of a military character, between the places where the coins were issued and those where they were found: they would not be passed from hand to hand from East to West of the Empire through districts in which they were not current coin, but would be more likely to come by sea, to be rejected at the first place where the holders had a chance of trying to negotiate them. The same phenomenon occurs in other provinces as well as in Britain—for instance, the finding in Syria of several coins struck by Peloponnesian cities about 200 A.D. has been explained, probably rightly, as due to the recruiting of troops in the Peloponnesus

for the Parthian War under Caracalla. Later, however, when the Roman currency had broken down in the fifth and sixth centuries, almost any piece of metal seems to have been accepted in the provinces as the equivalent of money, just as counters were used for fractional currency in England in the reign of Elizabeth; and this may explain the not infrequent occurrence of Byzantine bronze coins in England, where they could have no real status as currency. Byzantine gold, which is also found here, is of course in a different category, as it would possess a bullion value.

13. The meaning of casual finds of silver as well as of gold must be considered as quite distinct from that of finds of bronze: the bronze coinages of Greece and Rome were in nearly all cases merely token issues, whose metal value was small in proportion to their face value, whereas the silver and gold had an intrinsic value as commodities more nearly related to their denominations; and this would cause them to circulate outside the areas in which they were current coin. Casual finds of silver in particular occur in districts far from the place of issue, and are useful for tracing lines of trade. Where foreign silver coins are found sporadically in some quantity, it may be assumed in most cases that this district was one which had no native supplies of silver and imported the metal in exchange for its own products: this is noticeable, for instance, in North Germany and the Baltic lands, where considerable finds of Roman silver have been made: as a rule

the coins are in worn condition, often quite illegible, so that they would have lost any face value that they originally possessed, and they can only be supposed to have been traded as metal. A special class of casual finds of foreign silver may be mentioned, which is characteristic of the Hellenistic age, when large numbers of mercenary troops were recruited by the kings: in such districts as Crete, a favourite recruiting ground, there is evidence from finds of coins that when they returned home the soldiers brought with them the silver that had been issued to them as pay during their service. Gold, as it was more an article of luxury, is less indicative of trade connexions: a good many of the late Roman gold coins, especially the large gold medallions characteristic of the fourth century A.D., were probably sent as presents or subsidies to the barbarian chiefs on the borders of the Empire, and consequently have a political rather than a commercial significance.

14. When the meaning of casual finds of coins is considered, it must be remembered that the spot where a coin is found is not always that where it was originally lost. In the great majority of cases, no doubt, any accumulation of coins indicates a place of common resort or trade, especially if the coins are of varying denominations and cover a considerable period of time: it would be natural, for instance, that in a market-place all sorts of currency would be lost, as they are known to have been in mediæval fair-grounds

and in modern open-air markets, in the general litter. But there was probably in ancient times, as there is now, some shifting of the rubbish from the market-places to be used as manure on the fields in the vicinity; and this may explain the occasional occurrence of large numbers of Roman coins in areas which appear never to have been occupied as anything but cultivated fields. In such cases some clue to the origin of the coins may be deduced from other objects associated with them: if the place was a fair-ground, there will possibly be some small articles such as fibulae, which would be lost almost as easily as coins, amongst the finds; but rubbish used as manure would probably contain, as such rubbish does to-day in places where it is carted from ashpits to be spread on the fields, little that is not perishable except broken glass and pottery and small coins. Another agent in the shifting of coins from their original place of deposit is water: a stream which eats away its banks, if it passes through a Roman site, may wash out coins or similar relics and carry them for some distance down its course, till they are caught in some hole: if a pocket of this kind is discovered, it shows that traces of occupation should be found in the vicinity of the stream, but it may be necessary to search a long way up the banks. One of the most fruitful sources of Roman and British coins in this country about sixty years ago was on the coast of Sussex at Selsey, where an old man used to gather them by sifting the sand in certain hollows of the clay substratum near low-water-mark: there had been much erosion of the shore in the neighbourhood, and it was evident, from the explanation he gave me, that an old occupation site of Romano-British times had been washed away, and the coins had gradually worked their way down the shifting surface of the shore till they were caught in a hollow of a stiffer soil. The supply seems to have come to an end now, so presumably the whole of the site has been eroded.

15. In this connexion it may be remarked that the general character of the coins found in such cases as those described or as apparently casual losses may give a clue to the circumstances in which they were deposited. At Selsey the coins were nearly all gold or silver, such as would not be likely to be lost in any numbers, but would be kept in the houses of their owners; and this clearly suggests that the land eroded was the site of a house or houses of some importance. If the stray coins found scattered about a field are of small size and low value, the rubbish theory is a more probable explanation of their origin: they were dropped, and the owner did not notice his loss, or did not think it worth his while to make a search for them, and so they were in due course swept up and carried away. Sometimes forged or plated coins are found associated with other pieces of little value: here the presumption is in favour of a market-place or fairground, especially if the forgeries are numerous: the bad money would be thrown away by those who

detected its character, instead of being nailed to the counter as in more modern times. As a rule, coins of substantial value do not occur casually, except on house-sites, and then under conditions approximating to those of hoards: Roman denarii and sestertii are found singly here and there, but they only suggest that someone passed that way in Roman times and dropped a coin without noticing his loss. When several such coins are found scattered about a spot which does not appear to have been a house-site, it is usually interesting to seek for an explanation of their presence: for instance, the ground at the mouth of a cave in Derbyshire produced several sestertii, though the nearest Roman settlement is some distance away: it is possible that the cave was a show-place in those days, as it is now, and the coins may have been deposited as offerings. Such ideas are, of course, speculative, but it is often useful to advance them and to test them in relation to any other evidence that may be available.

16. When any information in regard to stratification can be secured in regard to a find of coins—this is rare except when they have been scientifically excavated—the value is normally greater in respect of a casual find than of a hoard. In cases of hoards deliberately secreted it might often happen that the hoarder dug a hole in the ground, put his coins into it, and tried to disguise the hole: the more successful the disguise, the more chance there would be of the hoard remaining undisturbed below the contemporary level

of stratification to puzzle an excavator. Casual losses might be disturbed by physical accidents: the agency of water has already been mentioned; and if a coin is dropped on sand or loose soil, it has a tendency to work down, especially if it is small: this tendency may be aided by burrowing creatures. Rubbish mounds are hopeless as regards stratification: in most parts of the Greek and Roman worlds they probably grew with a sort of wave action, as they do in the East to-day, and from time to time the top of the mound would curl over and some old deposits would slide down on more recent layers, in which event objects such as coins would be likely to roll out of their previous surroundings. But if a casual find is not in a collection of rubbish or in obviously made ground or loose soil, there is a reasonable probability that it was lost where it was found, and in such cases stratification becomes an important element in the evidence.

17. Despite all these difficulties, however, the amount of information, especially on the economic side of history, that can be derived from casual finds is very considerable. In Greek countries in particular the tabulation of such finds will throw light on the commercial, and sometimes on the political, connexions of the community in whose country they were discovered. Bronze, as has been mentioned, was much more local in its circulation than silver, and as a rule the list of coins from the site of a Greek city will show at least half of the bronze as of the issue

of that city or of the state to which it belonged, while the rest come from the country round, the number from each place of issue diminishing as the distance increases or the facility of communication decreases. To a less extent, the same principle applies in regard to small silver: before the fourth century B.C., it is rare to find any silver coin of lower denomination than a drachma far from its home, and even drachmas were not often exported from cities which struck any larger denomination: till the fifth century, indeed, it may be said that the bulk of the inter-state trade of Greece was transacted by means of the staters of a few central markets, while most cities only struck half-drachmas and obols for home consumption. In this period casual finds of staters, even more than hoards, supply evidence of commercial connexions, the importance of which can be judged to some extent by the number of finds. There is not the same amount of economic meaning to be read into finds of Roman coins after the foundation of the Empire, partly because there was only one currency and consequently not the same material for tracing the course of trade, partly because the distribution of coins in the Empire was probably effected in the main through military channels: supplies of coin were sent from Rome and put into circulation through being paid out to the soldiers.

18. The casual finds on a Greek or Roman site are of course useful for dating the length of its occupation, though the lower date may sometimes be more

definitely fixed than the upper: coins have a tendency to linger in circulation, and, as noted above, they may be found on a site to which they were not brought, probably, till two or three centuries after the date when they were struck. But if the finds are at all numerous, they should give a fairly close date for the occupation of the site: for instance, at a military station the series of coins will usually go back some years before it was constructed, beginning with worn specimens: the average number for each year will probably increase, and the average condition improve, up to a point at which freshly struck coins appear, after which the annual total should be more constant. This is an idealized scheme, but if the table of casual finds shows an approximation to it, the point specified may be taken as giving the date of occupation. On the other hand, if the abandonment of a site was gradual, the coin-finds will probably diminish as the population decreased, but may cease some time before the last inhabitants left: a decaying village would have proportionally less money in circulation than a busy one, and if the remnant of the population migrated in the end to a better home, they would take what possessions they could with them. But if a sudden and catastrophic fate befell a town, the coins found on the site will probably go on steadily to the date of destruction, and that date may be clearly marked: if some numbers of coins, including a proportion in fresh condition, are found in the ruins of a group of houses, as for instance at Cheddar, it may be concluded that the houses were sacked by raiders and that the raid was soon after the date of the latest coin found.

19. Greek coins also give a good deal of topographical information, if their find-spots are properly recorded, for the reasons explained in the last paragraph but one. If the site of a town is not known, but coins bearing its name have been found, the find-spots of these coins will furnish clues to its position: they can be plotted on a map, and the focal point of the finds will almost certainly be near the site wanted: if in a given area the small silver and bronze of an unknown city exceed in number all other issues, the city can safely be ascribed to that area. Large silver, as mentioned before, was apt to wander further: but unknown cities are not likely to have struck large silver coins.

NOTES

On most of the questions treated in this book, reference should be made to G. F. Hill's *Handbook of Greek and Roman Coins*, and it therefore seems unnecessary to mention the individual points and relevant pages. It may also be taken for certain that any hoard of Greek coins cited is described in S.P. Noe's Bibliography, the indices to which make it easy to trace each hoard or group of hoards, and references to Noe have been reduced to a minimum.

The abbreviations used in the notes are the following:

B.C.H.	*Bulletin de Correspondance Hellénique.*
B.M.C.	*British Museum Catalogue of Coins.*
B.N.J.	*British Numismatic Journal.*
C.A.C.A.M.	*Catalogue of Alexandrian Coins in the Ashmolean Museum.*
Gardner.	P. Gardner, *A History of Ancient Coinage*, 700–300 B.C.
Greek Coinage.	J. G. Milne, *Greek Coinage.*
Greek Development.	„ „ *The First Stages in the Development of Greek Coinage.*
H.N.	B. V. Head and others, *Historia Numorum*, ed. 2.
I.G.	*Inscriptiones Graecae.*
J.E.A.	*Journal of Egyptian Archaeology.*
J.H.S.	*Journal of Hellenic Studies.*
J.I.A.N.	*Journal International d'Archéologie Numismatique.*
J.R.S.	*Journal of Roman Studies.*
Michel.	C. Michel, *Recueil d'Inscriptions Grecques.*
N.C.	*Numismatic Chronicle.*
N.N.M.	*Numismatic Notes and Monographs.*
Noe.	S. P. Noe, *Bibliography of Greek Coin-hoards*, ed. 2.
R.N.	*Revue Numismatique.*
Roman Development.	J. G. Milne, *The Development of Roman Coinage.*
Z.f.N.	*Zeitschrift für Numismatik.*

GREEK AND ROMAN COINS

I.

2. The argument of this and the two following paragraphs is more fully set out in Greek Development.

The act of stamping a mark on a lump of metal, and so producing a ' coin', does not in itself endow the coin with a currency-value : as Aristotle explains (*Politics*, i. 9), the stamp in the first instance was merely a trademark. His examples of the kinds of commodities which were employed in primitive trade as a medium of exchange, silver and iron, show that he was thinking of the period before coinage (the early iron currency was in bars, not in coins), and primarily of European Greece (he does not mention the most important medium of the Asiatic cities, electrum).

3. The legend on the Lydian coins was formerly taken to be the name of Alyattes, but W. H. Buckler has shown this to be an error (J.H.S., xlvi. 36). It may be a place-name.

4. The statement in Greek Development that the drachma-weight was introduced by Pheidon requires correction: it was probably invented by Solon.

5. The common factor in the three main Greek standards was the drachma, which was a term of value, not a weight, when the standards were fixed, and was used only in Greece, where it was conventionally represented by a handful of iron rods : the amount of silver in a drachma-coin would be determined by the result of bargaining between the producers of silver and the markets where the coin was used. But the determination would be made at a place where the drachma was recognized as a term of value.

6. For fuller details, see Roman Development.

II.

2. Herodotus (vi. 46) states that the Thasians got more from the mainland than from the island, and refers to the exhausted workings: Thucydides (i. 100) refers only to mines on the mainland as in Thasian hands.

3. On coinage of Croesus see Greek Coinage, p. 11.

A. B. West (N.N.M., 40) dates the first Thasian issue to about

NOTES

411 B.C.: the weights of both silver and gold coins of the cities of the Thracian coast are irregular, and possibly no ratio of values was fixed, but the two metals were struck independently at weights suited to the convenience of the markets for which they were destined. So far as any correspondence with outside standards can be traced in these issues, they seem to be related to those of Asia: except during the Athenian Empire, most of the metal trade of Thasos was with the west coast of Asia Minor from the sixth to the fourth century.

4. On Sicilian gold, see Gardner, p. 405. The Athenian gold is discussed by West, p. 170.

5. The values of Cyzicenes at Athens and at Panticapaeum respectively appear from the statement of Demosthenes (xxxiv. in Phorm., 27). Demosthenes distorts the meaning of the exchange differences, probably to mislead the jury.

6. Greek traders with the Euxine do not seem to have dealt in gold to any great extent before the fourth century: probably the Scythians got a better market in the Persian empire.

7. The inventories of the temple of Delos illustrate the currency of the Aegaean area in the third and second centuries B.C.: older issues of gold, such as darics, lingered in the treasury, but Alexandrines are the most numerous.

9. See Greek Coinage, p. 12 on fifth century electrum issues. Lampsacene gold (i.e. electrum) is mentioned in Athenian treasury lists, but few specimens have survived.

The Phocaea-Mytilene inscription is Michel 8.

Cyzicene staters are frequently mentioned in the Athenian treasury-lists, and occur at Delos as late as 279 B.C. (Michel 833). The Phocaean name lasted longer as applied to impure gold, not only at Delos, but in Egypt (J.E.A., xx. 193).

10. An isolated issue of electrum occurred at Thebes about 395 B.C., but it does not seem to have been related to the ordinary Greek currency, and may have been an emergency coinage. There are traces of Asiatic influence (G. F. Hill, *Historical Greek Coins*, p. 63), and the electrum may have been obtained by melting down Cyzicenes.

The gold and electrum coins of Carthage were probably not issued simultaneously, though they may have been current together: W. Giesecke (*Antikes Geldwesen*, p. 84) dates the first gold 311–278, the electrum 277–211, the revived gold 190–146. The later Byzantine emperors certainly struck nomismata of different metals concurrently: Alexius I had four sets, in gold, electrum, billon, and bronze.

Kings of Bosporus: H.N., p. 504.

11. Recent research has shown that Chalcis probably played a more important part in the currency system of Greece about 600 B.C. than was supposed: see note in J.H.S., lviii. 96.

12. The accounts of the mining areas in O. Davies, *Roman Mines in Europe*, contain much information about the workings in the Greek period: particular attention should be given to his section on Laureium. For the Paeonian mines, see J. M. F. May, *The Coinage of Damastium*.

13. For a discussion of Spanish silver in relation to Greek trade, see N.C.5, xviii, 47.

14. See Roman Development, and in regard to mines O. Davies as above.

16. W. Giesecke, *Sicilia Numismatica*, gives the fullest account of Sicilian bronze.

17. See, J.E.A. xxiv. 200, on Ptolemaic bronze currency.

18. The dates given here are explained in Roman Development.

Under the Empire alternatives for the old Republican bronze alloy were used, an almost pure copper and a copper-zinc alloy known as orichalcum, possibly for convenience in distinguishing denominations: they do not seem to have been rated at metal values.

19. On Egyptian leaden currency see C.A.C.A.M., p. xliv. There is some evidence that a semi-official leaden currency was used in Palestine in the third century A.D.: this will shortly be published in *Iraq*.

Some of the tin coinages which have been reported may have been in fact cores for plating: compare *Iraq*, v. 21.

III.

1. Lesbian base silver: H.N., 558; B.M.C. Troas, p. 150.
2. Polycrates: Herodotus, iii. 56. Plated Lesbian electrum: e.g.

NOTES

B.M.C., *Troas, Lesbos* 76, 105, 112. Mytilene-Phocaea agreement: Michel 8. Themistocles at Magnesia: H.N., p. 581; Hill, *Hist. Greek Coins*, p. 45. Phoenician plated coins: B.M.C. *Phoenicia*, p. cxxix (re Tyre). Athenian plated coins: H.N., p. 373. Aeginetan and Corinthian plated coins have not been listed, but examples can be seen in most large collections.

    3. An extensive series of analyses of ancient coins is given in Z.f.N., xxvi. 1, by J. Hammer (*Feingehalt der griech. und rom. Münzen*).

    On the Roman plating, see H. Mattingly, *Roman Coins*, p. 93.

    4. Plated Alexandrine gold: *Iraq*, v. 20.

    5. See C. H. V. Sutherland, *Coinage and Currency in Roman Britain*, p. 42, on cast coins.

A distinction must be drawn between forgeries and another class of copies. Forgeries are direct reproductions, as close to the originals in appearance as the makers were capable of getting them, which were fraudulently intended to pass as official coins, to the profit of the issuers: they are normally contemporary with the coins they imitate. But many ' copies ' were issued without fraudulent intent, to meet emergencies or supply a currency where none existed, for which the types of coins known in the district were adopted: in such cases little attempt was made, as a rule, to produce exact facsimiles: they were, in fact, tokens, and the familiar types were regarded as marking denominations. They were probably issued under the sanction of whatever authority existed, and were often copied and recopied, with progressive deterioration, for an indefinite period.

IV.

    1. Minoan dumps: A. J. Evans, *Corolla Numismatica*, p. 363. G. F. Hill's account of ancient methods of coining in N.C.5, ii. 1, is particularly valuable in regard to the dies: see also next two notes.

    5. Casting of flans: Hill, p. 6. Strip metal: Hill, p. 11.

    6. Old coins re-used: Hill, p. 12. The only example of a Greek silver ingot comes from a hoard found at Tarentum, and was probably stamped at Selinus: see E. Babelon, *Trouvaille de Tarente*, in R.N., 1912, p. 32; also N.C.5, xviii. 49.

GREEK AND ROMAN COINS

Microscopical tests: C. F. Elam, *Journal of Institute of Metals*, xlv. 57.

Weights of Corinthian line of trade: N.C.5, iv. 29.

7. Persian standard in Ionia: N.C.5, iv. 19. Restruck Alexandrines: ib. 24. Some of the coastal Asiatic mints, notably Rhodes and Chios, instead of restriking the coins of Alexander, struck with his types, adding the badge of the city and the name of the responsible magistrate.

8. Restruck bronze of Smyrna: N.C.5, viii. 110. Hoard of coins as blanks: G. F. Hill, *Essays in Honour of W.Ridgeway*, p. 110.

9. The war-loot from the Spanish campaigns of the early years of the second century included large quantities of coins, Roman bigati and Spanish argentum Oscense, and the latter might be melted down for recoinage; but there is no evidence that the produce of the Spanish mines, after they came under Roman control, was turned into coin before it was sent to Rome.

Composition of Roman hoards of denarii: see Tables of finds in B.M.C. *Roman Republic*, vol. iii: also ii. 321.

10. Bean-shaped coins: e.g. B.M.C., *Ionia*, plates i–iii. Square coins: see B.M.C., *India, Greek and Scythic kings*: the Indian influence is shown by the fact that the use of square bronze flans comes in with the introduction of Indian legends alongside of Greek. Rectangular bricks: e.g. B.M.C., *Roman Republic*, plates i–iv. Fish-shaped coins: H.N., p. 272. Agrigentine bronze: H.N., p. 120.

V.

2. Greek dies: G. F. Hill, N.C.5, ii. 14. Joint user of dies: K. Regling, Z.f.N., xxiii. 101; N.C.5, xviii. 63.

3. Die-positions: G. Macdonald, *Fixed and loose dies in ancient coinage*, in *Corolla Numismatica*, p. 178. Alexandrian die-positions: C.A.C.A.M., p. xlii.

4. Cracked dies: Hill, N.C.5, ii. 24. Alexandrian die-life: N.C.4, x. 338. Corinthian dies: O. Ravel, R.N., 1932, p. 1.

5. Die-positions (at Smyrna): N.C.4 xvii, 315. Arab dies: G. Marçais, *Annales de l'Institut d'Etudes Orientales*, 1936, p. 180.

6. Dies at Athens: M. L. Kambanis, B.C.H., 1912, p. 44. Dies at Aradus: *Iraq*, v. 18. Dies at Alexandria Troas: H. von Fritze, *Nomisma*, vi. 24.

NOTES

7. Dies of Tiberius: C. H. V. Sutherland, J.R.S., xxviii. 136.
Mediaeval English dies: H. B. Earle Fox and J. Shirley Fox,
B.N.J., vi. 197.

VI.

1. The art of Greek coins can be studied in the plates of the
British Museum Guide to the Principal Coins of the Greeks: this
obviates the need of any illustrations here.

2. The standing of artistic coinages in Greece is best treated by
K. Regling in *Die antike Münze als Kunstwerk.*

Aristophanes: Frogs 722.

The Maria Theresa dollar has just been demonetized in
Abyssinia.

3. Coinage of the Eleians: N.C.5, xi. 171.

5. Cretan coinages: H.N., p. 457. For illustrations, see J. N.
Svoronos, *Numismatique de la Crète ancienne*, plates v (Cnossus)
and xii–xiv (Gortyna).

Hubbing: Hill, N.C.5, ii. 19. The most probable instances of
hubbing in Greek coins are from Italy and Sicily: in a few Greek
and Eastern mints the main part of the design may have been
hubbed from a master die, and details added in retouching, but
if the Greek artists were able to reproduce a design with the
precision of a Chinese artist, this would explain the close similarity
of dies. The Romans may have learnt the idea from their
Greek neighbours in South Italy, and in the Imperial coinages the
hubbing of the obverse types at any rate would have been worth
while. In the ordinary Greek city state, where perhaps only one
or two dies were required in a year, there would have been no
advantage in the practice.

6. Roman provincial imitations: C. H. V. Sutherland,
N.N.M., 65.

VII.

1. The history and meaning of coin types should be studied
in G. Macdonald, *Coin Types, their Origin and Development.*

Signets as types: H.N., p. 571. The one name on an early
Greek coin, that of Phanes, is almost certainly that of a merchant:

kings did not put their names on their coins, with the one exception of Getas, King of the Edonians, before the Persian War.

2. Magistrates' names: e.g. at Abdera, H.N., p. 254; at Maroneia, H.N., p. 249.

6. Zancle-Messana: H.N., p. 152. Orchomenus: H.N., p. 346. Abdera: H.N., p. 253.

7. Copies of Athenian types: early, J. N. Svoronos, *Trésor des Monnaies d'Athènes*, plates 2–7; eastern, E. T. Newell, N.N.M., 82; Arabian, B.M.C., *Mesopotamia*, etc., p. xlv; Cretan, H.N., p. 462.

8. Corinthian colonies: H.N., 406. Pegasus in Illyria: J. von Schlosser, *Beschreibung der Altgriechischen Münzen, Wien*, p. 70, 1; at Emporiae: H.N., p. 2.

9. Byzantium and Chalcedon: G. F. Hill, *Handbook of Greek and Roman Coins*, p. 106. Ephesus and Aradus: H.N., p. 575.

10. Cyzicene types: H.N., p. 523. Compare the coinage of Melos, discussed in N.N.M., 62, p. 7.

11. The 'Homonoia' coins normally have the Emperor's head on the obverse: i.e. they belong to the class of Asiatic Imperial issues which was rather medallic in its types: the 'pseudautonomous' series struck at several cities without the head or name of an Emperor, with more commonplace types, and generally of smaller size, probably supplied the chief commercial bronze currency when Roman issues were insufficient.

12. See Roman Development for fuller details.

VIII.

1. Athens mint: I.G., ii. 476, 30.

2. Mytilene-Phocaea agreement: Michel, 8.

3. The shopmarks of the Roman and provincial mints are definite in the latter part of the third century and throughout the fourth: there were probably privy marks before that time, but the scheme has not yet been unravelled: compare the possible shopmarks in the Roman mint at Alexandria, J.R.S., viii. 154.

5. Aradus: *Iraq*, v. 12. Alexandria: C.A.C.A.M. Tables.

7. Roman gold hoard: *Notizie d. Scavi*, 1899, p. 327. Alexandria under Tiberius: N.C.4, x. 337.

NOTES

IX.

1. Fancy engraving or marking of coins by irresponsible individuals was done in ancient as in modern times, but need not be considered.

A good deal of silver was countermarked in Crete, usually with a stamp which has been explained as representing a lebes. A notable series of countermarks occurs on the late silver of Side: see R. Mowat in *Corolla Numismatica*, p. 189.

Earlier series restamped: silver, e.g. Sinope, *Recueil Waddington*, pl. xxv, 32, 33, 37; bronze, e.g. Erythrae, B.M.C., *Ionia*, pl. xvi, 8.

Aristophanes: Eccl. 819: compare Gortyna inscription, J.I.A.N., 1898, p. 165.

2. Imperial Greek bronze: Imhoof-Blumer, *Griechische Münzen*, p. 157.

3. Roman Imperial: B.M.C., *Roman Empire*, i. p. xxviii. The effect of this procedure was probably like that of an English confirmation by a writ of Inspeximus.

4. Lydia: B.M.C., *Lydia*, p. 2, 5; p. 3, 14, 15, 19, 20. Elis: N.C.5, xi. 177. Aegina: B.M.C., *Attica*, p. 127, 15, 17; p. 128, 32–38; p. 133, 95–104. Persia: B.M.C., *Mesopotamia*, etc., p. cxxxvi.

Aramaic marks: C. C. Torrey, N.N.M., 77.

Tenian inscription: I.G., xii, 817. H.N., p.493.

X.

2. The action of Pheidon simply amounted to an order that Aeginetan staters should be accepted in the districts under his control at a fixed value: there was no need to have coins struck with his own name or badge.

4. Solon's reform: J.H.S., i, 179 and lviii, 96.

6. Thracian weights: H.N., p. xlii.

7. Sicily: N.C.5, xviii, 47.

8. Persian standard: N.C.5, iv. 19.

9. Phoenician standards: *Iraq*, v. 12.

GREEK AND ROMAN COINS

10. Cyrenaica: B.M.C. *Cyrenaica*, p. ccviii.
11. Ptolemaic currency: J.E.A., xxiv, 200.

XI.

4. Egyptian dated hoards: e.g. *Karanis Reports*, 1924–31, p. 60.
5. Early hoards: e.g. Noe, 920 (Santorin), 1052 (Tarentum), 323 (Demanhur), 851 (Ras Shamra), 144 (Beni Hasan), 143 (Benha). In the last-named, nearly all the coins were cut; in the last but one, only the Phoenician.
6. Delos accounts: e.g. Michel, 815, 833. Egyptian temple hoard: J.E.A., xxi. 211.
8. Demanhur hoard: Noe, 324.
9. Robbers' hoard: e.g. A. O. Curle, *The Treasure of Traprain*.
11. Greek bronze in England: N.C.5, xvii. 124. Procolitia: *Proceedings of Soc. of Antiquaries, Newcastle*, 4, vii. 191. Amulets: N.C.5, xiii. 85.
12. Syrian finds: H. Seyrig in *Syria*, xvii. 174.
13. German finds: S. Bolin, *Fynden av Romerska Mynt i det fria Germanien*: compare for French finds A. Blanchet, *Les trésors de monnaies romaines et les invasions germaniques du Gaule*.
14. Woodeaton was probably a fair-ground: J.R.S., xxi. 101.

There are many places in England where the deposit of rubbish is altering the nature of what may come to be archæological evidence: an estate which I knew as a grouse-moor is now covered with rubbish tipped from a city some miles distant.

17. For examples of lists of coins, see K. Regling, *Münzfunde aus Pergamon*, and *American School at Athens Reports, Corinth*, vol. vi.

KEY TO PLATES

[The dates given are all B.C., except that Roman Imperial issues are dated by reigns of emperors.]

Plate I. DEVELOPMENT OF THE OBVERSE DIE (§IV, 1).

1. Dump punched on striated surface: Ionian, probably early eighth century.
2. Surface made into die by deepening striations into geometric design: North Ionian, probably late eighth century.
3. Geometric design replaced by badge of heraldic character: probably Samos, early seventh century.
4. Also a badge: possibly Parium, seventh century.
5. Another badge: probably Cyme (Aeolis), seventh century.
6 and 7. Lion's head badge of Mermnadae, with parts of Lydian legend: Lydia, late seventh century.
8. Elaborated heraldic device: Ionian, early sixth century.
9. Fully developed archaic style: Chios, c.500.

Plate. II EXCEPTIONAL DIE-FABRICS (§ IV, 2, 3).

1. Reverse of flat surface with sketchy design in low relief: Derrones (Thrace), late sixth century.
2. Similar reverse: Populonia (Etruria), middle fifth century.
3. Reverse design an incuse repetition of that on obverse, minor details omitted: Tarentum, sixth century.
4. Similar repetition of design, with different names on the two faces: Siris and Pyxus, sixth century.
5. Same fabric, with different designs on the two faces: Croton and Sybaris, sixth century.

121

GREEK AND ROMAN COINS

Plate III. DEVELOPMENT OF REVERSE DIE IN GREECE (§ IV, 4).

1. Broad-faced hammer with central design: Corinth, c.600.
2. Small punch with flat margin: Thebes, c.500.
3. Square punch die without margin: Thebes, c.480.
4 and 5. Punch expanded and made rounder: Thebes, c.440 and 400.
6. Reverse die covering whole flan: Thebes, c.370.
7. Normal form of late reverse die: Boeotian League, c.270.

Plate IV. OVERSTRUCK COINS SHOWING TRACES OF ORIGINAL TYPES (§ IV, 6).

1. Obverse with remains of Pegasus type (wing and head clearest), reverse with traces of swastica, from Corinthian coin like Pl. III, 1: Metapontum, sixth century.
2. Similar traces: Caulonia, sixth century.
3. Showing outlines of Athenian types from a coin like Pl. V, 1: Cyrene, sixth century.
4. With remains of types of Abdera of same period as Pl. VII, 3 (clearest, the magistrate's symbol, a cock, on obverse): Aenus, fifth century.
5. With flattened outline of Aeginetan turtle like Pl. V, 7 on obverse: Lyttus, fifth century.

Plate V. CONSERVATISM OF TYPES IN COMMERCIAL COINAGES (§ VI, 2).

1 to 3. Showing little artistic advance: Athens, sixth, fifth, and fourth centuries.
4 to 6. With the same main types but considerable artistic improvement: Corinth, sixth, fifth, and fourth centuries.
7. A type practically unaltered from the beginning of the seventh century to the middle of the fifth: Aegina, sixth century.

KEY TO PLATES

Plate VI. CHOICE OF TYPES (§ VII, 1).

1. An electrum coin, with a stag and the legend 'I am the badge of Phanes': Ionian, late seventh century.
2. With a lion's mask, a known city badge: Samos, early sixth century.
3. With a seal, also a known badge: Phocaea, same period.
4. With a figleaf, similarly known: Camirus (Rhodes), same period.
5. The only one illustrated from this period which bears the name of the issuing city: Ephesus, late sixth century.
6. Another known type: Lampsacus, c.500.
7, 8, and 9 belong to a group of coins struck at the end of the seventh and beginning of the sixth centuries for currency in Euboea and Attica at a central mint, probably Chalcis; the bull's head is probably for Euboea generally, the Gorgoneion may be for Eretria, the wheel is certainly of Chalcis. None of the foregoing bears a type on the reverse.
10. Has the head of Athene joined as a reverse type to the city badge on the obverse: Methymna (Lesbos), early fifth century.
11. Similarly has the head of Aphrodite: Cnidus, c.500.

Plate VII. MAGISTRATES' BADGES AND NAMES (§ VII, 2).

1. With two badges, dolphin and eagle's head: Corinth, late fifth century.
2. With shield as badge: Thasos, late fifth century.
3. With satyr as badge and abbreviated name: Abdera, early fifth century.
4 and 5. With name in full, but in eponymous form: Abdera and Maroneia, fourth century.
6. Showing fullest development of control by names and badges, three names of magistrates with the badge of one in the field, a month-letter (on the amphora), and an abbreviated name below: Athens, second century.

123

GREEK AND ROMAN COINS

Plate VIII. SICILIAN TYPES (§ VII, 3).

1. A crab, as a local product: Acragas, c.520.
2. A leaf of the wild parsley from which the city was named: Selinus, c.580.
3. A dolphin in a sickle-shaped mole, symbolizing the harbour: Zancle-Messana, c.540.
4. With head of Dionysus and bunch of grapes, advertizing the vineyards of the district: Naxos, c.510.
5. With Satyr washing himself, advertizing the baths of the city: Himera, c.430.
6. With topical allusions to the refoundation of the city under a new name by Hieron I in the head of Silenus, the slave of Polyphemus, and the Aetnaean beetle below it: Catana-Aetna, c.475.
7. With the mule-car of Anaxilas of Rhegium, a type transferred to Messana after it came under his control: Messana, c.480.
8. With a modification of an old horseman type revived probably to commemorate the share of the Geloan cavalry in the defeat of the Athenian expedition to Sicily: Gela, c.410.

Plate IX. COMMEMORATIVE MEDALLIONS (§ VII, 3).

1. The Damareteion, struck after the victory of Gelon over the Carthaginians at Himera: Syracuse, c.480.
2. A decadrachm probably commemorating the final expulsion of the Persian armies from Greece: Athens, c.480.
3. The historical relations of which have not been identified: Acragas, c.430.

Plate X. PERSONAL ELEMENT IN ROMAN REPUBLICAN TYPES (§ VII, 4).

1. With the finding of Romulus and Remus by the shepherd Faustulus, linking the family with legend: Sex. Pompeius Fostlus, c.150.

124

KEY TO PLATES

2. With the death of Tarpeia at the hands of the Sabines, a similar link: L. Titurius Sabinus, c.85.

3. With the return home of Ulysses, claimed as an ancestor by the Mamilii: C. Mamilius Limetanus, c.85.

4. With the traditional method of oath-taking: Ti. Veturius, c.90.

5. With column said to have been erected in honour of an ancestor in 439: C. Augurinus, c.145.

6. With the Puteal Scribonianum: L. Scribonius Libo, c.55.

7. With the triumph over Perseus of Macedonia in 168: P. Lepidus, c.70.

8. With a scene typifying the Romanization of Spain under Sertorius: A. Postumius Albinus, c.75.

9. Showing the moneyer's acceptance of the surrender of the Jewish leader Bacchius: A. Plautius, c.56.

10. With head of Scipio Africanus the elder, as a famous member of the house: Cn. Cornelius Blasio, c.100.

11. With portrait of Julius Caesar: M. Mettius, 44.

12. With head of a Gaul, possibly portrait of Vercingetorix: Hostilius Saserna, 48.

Plate XI. COPIES OF ATHENIAN TYPES (§ VII, 7).

1. Contemporary version of Athenian tetradrachm: possibly Thracian Chersonese, sixth century.

2. Barbarian, probably contemporary, imitation: North Arabia or Syria, middle fifth century.

3. Derivative copy of types: Central Asia, late fourth century.

4. Barbarous copy at several removes in lead: Palmyra, probably Roman period.

5. Late copy of types for unrelated currency: Southern Arabia, late second century.

6. Close contemporary copy differentiated only by name and symbol: Gortyna, second century.

GREEK AND ROMAN COINS

Plate XII. COPIES OF CORINTHIAN TYPES AND OTHER COMMERCIAL CORRESPONDENCES (§ VII, 8, 9).

1. Differentiated from Corinthian issues only by initial of city, from a Corinthian colony: Leucas, fourth century.
2. Similar, but from a city not founded by Corinth: Locri (Italy), fourth century.
3. With borrowing of Pegasus type: Illyria, probably late third century.
4. With similar borrowing: Emporiae, third century.
5 and 6. With closely similar main type on obverse: Byzantium and Chalcedon, fourth century.
7 and 8. With same types, obverse and reverse: Ephesus and Aradus, third/second century.

Plate XIII. SUGGESTIONS OF COMMERCIAL CONNEXION (§ VII, 10, 11).

1 to 6. Illustrating the wide range of types used for the Cyzicene electrum—Heracles, Apollo, Helios, head of nymph, Dionysus, eagle—with the tunny, the city badge, in a subordinate place: Cyzicus, fifth and fourth centuries.
7 and 8. Showing a similar range on the gold Lampsacenes (see § II, 5), which had the city badge, the sea-horse, on reverse: Lampsacus, fourth century.
9. Of the 'island' class of Aeginetan fabric: Carthaea (Ceos), seventh century.
10 to 12. Typical examples of the 'Homonoia' coins of Asia Minor, with designs conceived on ordinary lines: Smyrna with Lacedaemon, Commodus; Ephesus with Smyrna, Domitian; Smyrna with Pergamum, Caracalla.

Plate XIV. COUNTERMARKED COINS (§ IX, 1).

1. A silver coin of a series frequently found conspicuously stamped on both faces: Sinope, third century.
2. Also silver of a series frequently countermarked, but on one face only and with stamps of varying origin, for the most

126

KEY TO PLATES

part cistophoric mints of Asiatic cities: Side (Pamphylia), second century.

3 and 4. Bronze, marked on both faces with a star, both from the same series, but with different magistrates' names, which suggests that the reason here for countermarking was not the default of a particular magistrate: Erythrae, third century.

5. Bronze, similarly countermarked with a bee: Erythrae, first century.

6. Of a bronze series often countermarked with a head of Athene, characteristic of a later series: Clazomenae, second century.

7. Bronze, with an incuse letter as countermark, peculiar to this series: Clazomenae, third century.

8. Bronze, with a monogram which occurs as a magistrate's mark on a later series: Cyme (Aeolis), third century.

9. A very worn bronze coin, probably restamped on that account with a more elaborate countermark than usual, the twin Nemeses and part of the name of Smyrna: Smyrna, probably Sept. Severus.

10. Similar to last, but countermarked with Emperor's head and name of city: Smyrna, probably Sept. Severus.

Plate XV. COUNTERMARKED BRONZE COINS (§ IX, 2, 3).

1. Countermarked B to signify revaluation at 2 assaria: Smyrna, Caracalla.

2. Similarly revalued at 5 assaria: Side, Salonina.

3. Showing 'probation' of early Imperial period at Rome: IMPAVG on Augustus.

4. Similar: TIB on Augustus.

5. Similar: NCAPR on Antonia Claudii.

6. Legionary countermarking of coin of Sebaste in Palestine with badge and initials of Leg. X Fretensis beside other marks: Palestine, ? Hadrian.

7. Erasure of portrait of Geta after his murder: Stratonicea (Caria), Caracalla

127

GREEK AND ROMAN COINS

Plate XVI. PUNCHMARKED COINS (§ IX, 4).

1. Electrum third-stater punchmarked on the edge of the reverse: Lydia, seventh century.

2 and 3. Silver sigloi punched on obverse and reverse respectively: Persia, fourth century.

4 and 5. Silver staters both doubly punched on obverse: Elis, fifth century.

6. Silver tetradrachm repeatedly punched on both faces: Ptolemy II, c.270.

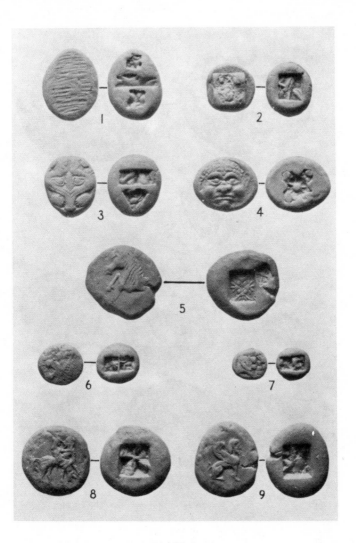

PLATE I

PLATE II

PLATE III

PLATE IV

PLATE V

PLATE VI

PLATE VII

PLATE VIII

PLATE IX

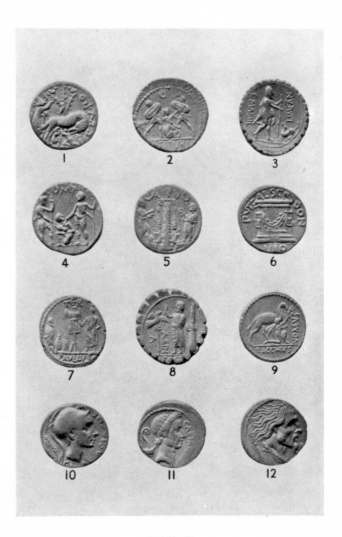

PLATE X

PLATE XI

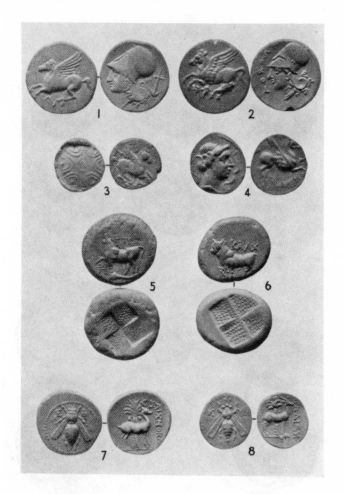

PLATE XII

PLATE XIII

PLATE XIV

PLATE XV

PLATE XVI